THE GENERAL STRIKE MAY 1926: TRADES COUNCILS IN ACTION

Prepared by
EMILE BURNS

for the

LABOUR RESEARCH DEPARTMENT
162 Buckingham Palace Road, London, S.W.1

1926

This edition published by
LAWRENCE & WISHART LTD.
46 Bedford Row, London, W.C.1

1975

Published 1926
This edition 1975

Printed in Great Britain by
The Camelot Press Ltd, Southampton

CONTENTS

CARTOONS, ETC., REPRODUCED.

THE GENERAL STRIKE, MAY 1926:
TRADES COUNCILS IN ACTION.

INTRODUCTION.

IN the " proposals for co-ordinated action " issued by the General Council to Union Executives on the night of April 30, and accepted by the conference of Union Executives on May 1, the following instructions were given to Trades Councils :—

" The work of the Trades Councils, in conjunction with the local officers of the trade unions actually participating in the dispute, shall be to assist in carrying out the foregoing provisions (*i.e.*, stoppage of work in various trades and undertakings, and exceptions thereto), and they shall be charged with the responsibility of organising the trade unionists in dispute in the most effective manner for the preservation of peace and order."

The purpose of this book is to examine the response made by the Trades Councils to these instructions, and to record the forms of local organisation and activity which were developed during the Nine Days.

But it is not merely as a historical record that the book has been prepared. The General Strike of May, 1926, cannot be regarded as an isolated event ; " Never Again " is the despairing prayer of individuals who do not like the course of events, rather than a serious judgment of what the course of events is likely to be. No one in the working-class movement can fail to realise that the conditions which led up to the General Strike are still in existence, and that they will continue so long as the capitalist organisation of society exists. The strike even of a single union on a national scale is a comparatively modern feature ; the widening of the conflict in the development of the class struggle is a simple historical fact.

Therefore the study of the local organisation and activities during the General Strike of May, 1926, is important in order that the working-class movement as a whole, and in particular the local organisations, may be able to learn the lessons of experience, and make the necessary preparations to deal effectively with any similar emergencies which may arise in the future.

The material for this book has been obtained from the most direct and authoritative source—the secretaries of the Trades Councils or other centralising local organisations where Trades Councils did not exist. Immediately after the General Strike a questionnaire was sent out to Trades Councils affiliated to the Labour Research Department, and later a similar questionnaire was sent to other Trades Councils and Labour Parties. The form of the questionnaire was as follows :—

GENERAL STRIKE—QUESTIONNAIRE.

When filled in, please return to L.R.D., 162 Buckingham Palace Road, London, S.W.1.

1. In what way did the local organisation act ?
    As Trades Council in ordinary form ?
    As Council of Action, including T.C. and Strike Committees ?
    Or any other form ?

2. Have any arrangements been made to keep the strike organisation in existence ?

3. Were any arrangements made with the Co-op., and in what form ?

4. Were there any special points in local organisation (good or bad) which are worth noting ?

5. Did you run a strike sheet or bulletin locally ?

 If so, which day was it started ?

 How many days was it issued ?

 How many copies daily ?

 Can you supply us with a set, or even a few copies ?

 Is it to be continued in any form ?

6. Was there any organisation of Workers' Defence Corps in any form ?

 How many arrests are known to have taken place locally ?

7. Was there any sign of weakening locally on May 12th ?

Signature..

Address..

....

Trades Council..

The replies received were, as might be expected, of very unequal length and value. To some extent this reflects the varying importance—from the point of view of organised activity—of the Trades Councils ; in any case the replies received form an invaluable record, though it is admittedly incomplete. We have considered the best method of presentation to be the actual words of the replies received, and not any form of summary which might obscure particular points;

The only modifications made have been the elimination of names of individuals, and the omission, for reasons of space, of replies which were purely negative.

In chapters preceding the actual reports, we have made a brief analysis of the reports under particular headings, so as to bring out the essential points in the replies ; and we have added a chapter giving a brief account of the problems of organisation and work now facing the Trades Councils.   In the treatment of each question an attempt has been made to select from the reports the most useful examples of organisation and activity, so that the experience of one Trades Council may be made available for others.   In some instances, also, local activities have been criticised and contrasted with those of other areas, but both criticisms and suggestions are based on a careful study of the various reports, and will, it is hoped, prove useful to those who are actively engaged in the work of building up the Trades Councils.

CHAPTER I.

THE COUNCILS OF ACTION.

AT the time when the General Council issued its call to Trades Councils, these bodies, taken as a whole, were organisations accustomed to monthly delegate meetings, with fortnightly or monthly meetings of Executive Committees. Practically in all cases there were no paid officials, and some even of the most energetic Councils had no premises of their own. With one or two exceptions which appear from the reports, no preparatory work of any kind had been undertaken before the call was issued. For all practical purposes, the Councils were organisations suddenly asked to take on a new and urgent task, without any but the vaguest suggestion of how they should carry it out. The work was carried out, and viewed as a whole it was carried out effectively. With very few exceptions indeed the Councils displayed energy and initiative to an extent that astonished all who had known them in the preceding period. Councils which had never had any real existence, Councils which were considered moribund, as well as normally active Councils—all seemed to get a sudden inspiration, developed new forms of organisation and activity, drew in numbers of new helpers and for the first time in their history— at any rate in their recent history—became the real expression of the local movement.

FORM OF ORGANISATION.

The first matter which had to be settled was the question of organisation—what form of controlling body should be set up, and through what machinery it should work. In some cases the initial meeting

was a specially summoned General Meeting of delegates, but in most cases it was a meeting of the Executive Committee of the Council, sometimes with the
addition of special individuals or representatives.   In
any case, it was apparent from the start that the
existing Trades Council could not function as it stood ;
within the Council's area there were many trade union
branches which were not affiliated, and also in many
cases the political organisations were distinct.   Further,
the General Council's instructions were to act in conjunction with the local organisations of the Unions
involved ; and these local organisations acted through
special strike committees, distinct from the branch
machinery which was represented on the Council by
branch delegates.   The essentials for successful work
in the emergency were wider representation and more
direct contact with the strike committees.

There was one experience on a national scale which
gave a definite pointer, and which accounts for the
similarity of the organisation set up more or less
simultaneously by the Trades Councils in every part
of the country.   In August, 1920, the formation of the
national Council of Action was accompanied by the
formation of local Councils of Action.   The Government's abandonment of the attack on Russia on that
occasion meant that the Councils of Action were never
called upon to act, and after a few weeks of purely
formal or propaganda meetings they " withered away."
But like every other experience the Councils of Action
of 1920 had left their mark, and in the emergency
of 1926 the Trades Councils turned instinctively to
that form of organisation, and even in many cases
used the name.   The following groups the names
under which the various special organisations (those
replying to the questionnaire) appear to have functioned, omitting indeterminate descriptions :—

Functioning as			*Number.*
Councils of Action,	...	...	54
Strike Committees,	...	...	45
Trades Councils,	...	...	15
Emergency Committees,		...	8
Other descriptions,	...	...	9
			131

Some of the other descriptions were " Disputes Advisory Council " (Aldershot), "Vigilance Committee " (Lincoln), and a few were described as " Industrial Committees."   Dunfermline reports :—

"A Council of Action was formed prior to the strike, but somehow great objection was made against the name, therefore we had to change the name to Strike Committee, under the direct control of our Council."

Except in a few cases, where the Strike Committees apparently refused any organised link with the Trades Council, the directing local organisation was in effect a Council of Action uniting all local labour organisations.   In two cases of those reporting (Croydon and Gateshead), the Trades Council formed a " Council of Action " which sent delegates to the local Central Strike Committee.   In such cases the use of the word Council of Action is misleading, as it was usually applied to the co-ordinating body, not to a subsidiary group.

CONSTITUENT ELEMENTS.

In the majority of cases where the composition of the Council of Action (or Central Strike Committee) is clearly stated, the constituent elements were :—

Trades Council representatives, usually the Executive Committee.

Strike Committee representatives from each of the Unions (or groups) involved.

> Representatives of other Unions not affiliated to the Trades Council.
>
> Representatives of special groups, such as the Labour Party where that organisation was distinct; Labour Councillors or Guardians, Women's Organisations, etc.

In other words, the Council of Action really united the whole of the organised Labour movement in the area, with the sole but fundamentally important exception of the Co-operative Societies. Co-operative Guilds were, of course, connected either directly or through the Trades Council or Labour Party; but only in a few cases is there any definite mention of Co-operative representatives. The full examination of this point belongs to another chapter; but the lack of connection with the Co-operative Societies was deplorable, and was the one black spot in the otherwise excellent basis of organisation.

It is not necessary to examine the various details of representation on the Councils of Action; in some cases the full basis of representation was settled from the start, while in others it was gradually developed. The only point of principle that emerges is that there was no standing order and no plan of organisation under which action could be taken automatically. But this is only one aspect of the lack of preparation which affected the whole situation.

There is, however, one other comment which must be made with regard to the central co-ordinating body. We have given above the normal composition of the Council of Action or Central Strike Committee. But there were exceptions. In some cases one or more of the Unions affected refused to co-operate with the Trades Council; in others the Central Strike Committee of the Unions involved did not apparently refuse to co-operate, but maintained a separate existence, even though there was representation from one body to the other.

At all times, and above all in an emergency such as the general strike, the refusal of any group to co-operate with the Trades Council—the embodiment of united organised Labour—deserves the strongest condemnation. Any section of the workers which deliberately stands apart in a struggle of this kind is acting not only shortsightedly but criminally, whatever reason it may give. No working-class organisation, however strong it may think itself, can stand alone; and if it thinks that the Trades Council is weak and ineffective, its duty to the movement is to go in and help it. Fortunately there were not very many cases; among the Trades Councils reporting, only one, Dorking, states that the Trades Council was ignored—" The N.U.R., being the largest unit, acted separately as a Strike Committee." Llandudno, however, seems to have been in the same position :—

" We were not called upon to act in any way. The Strike Centre was at Llandudno Junction. Railwaymen only in this district."

But this may merely mean lack of initiative on the part of the Trades Council. At Castle Cary also the N.U.R. branch apparently functioned as the sole Strike Committee—" the Trades Council did not officially function." Keighley mentions, " Rail Clerks aloofness from Strike Committee "—against which, however, must be set the special help given by the R.C.A. in other places. The unwillingness to co-operate sometimes took less acute forms, but was nevertheless evident. Dunfermline reports :—

" Certain Trade Unions seem to be afraid to put their business in the hands of the Trades Council; they stood aloof and information was very difficult to ascertain as to how they were progressing."

At Middlesbrough the Trades Council had to "go slow," owing to the attitude of some Trade Union delegates who feared interference by the Central Strike Committee with "domestic affairs"; but tactful handling seems to have been successful.

Edmonton calls attention to the difficulty of being a dormitory, resulting in lack of contact with trade unionists living there but belonging to central branches. The only solution is the affiliation by Unions of their residential membership in each area ; this is, of course, frequently done, but it could be much more general than it is at present. It is also possible that a developed system of grouping might lead to the attachment to the groups, for local purposes, of individual trade unionists whose branches meet outside the area in which they live.

To sum up the results of the foregoing examination, it can be said that the co-ordinating body in such an emergency must be a Council of Action or Joint Strike Committee composed of representatives of every section of the organised movement in the locality—industrial, political, co-operative. No narrower basis can express the real needs of the workers or be really effective. And this conclusion leads to another : the need to establish the Trades Councils on this basis in times of peace, so that they are ready, without delay or the possibility of friction, to act in any emergency that may arise. The unity and harmony reported by the majority of Trades Councils must become general, and must apply in the everyday work of the Councils, as well as in a General Strike. Fortunately, much of the spirit of the Nine Days has survived. Many Trades Councils report the affiliation of bodies hitherto unaffiliated, and in several areas a Trades Council has been formed where none existed before. It is essential to the movement that still greater progress should be made in this direction, until every Trades Council is a fully representative body maintaining regular contact with every Labour organisation in its area.

FUNCTIONS OF THE COUNCILS.

The detailed work done by the Councils is described in other chapters ; the purpose of this section is to examine the general nature of their activity—what the General Council intended they should do, how far the Councils extended their functions owing to the ne- cessities of the situation, and—arising out of the definite views expressed in the reports—what functions they should fulfil in such an emergency.

The vagueness of the General Council's instruction has already been indicated. The first duty placed upon the Trades Councils—of seeing that the in- structions for the stoppage were carried out correctly— was the source of a great deal of trouble and some friction, owing to the fact that the actual instructions to the trade union branches came from their own head offices. If a branch secretary had not received in- structions, his men were not called out, even if all other men working on the same job had been called out by other unions. The Council of Action could do nothing but try to get the instruction through ; it had no authority to tell the secretary to bring his men out, however clearly it was the General Council's intention that they should come out. A similar position arose where there was any doubt as to the interpretation of the Union's instruction. The Trades Council had no clear authority to settle the point, and had to act as an enquiry agency—trying to get the matter settled by a higher authority, the Union con- cerned or one of the General Council's sub-committees.

In fact, the Councils did, in many cases, settle such matters on their own initiative, mainly where the branch secretary concerned had the good sense to submit the question for interpretation by the Council or was prepared to act as the Council thought right. The usual source of trouble, however, was the desire of the workers who had not been called out to join their comrades on strike ;   many Councils had to spend considerable energy in persuading men to resume work.

The details, however, are not important ; what is important is the fact that confusion and difficulties did arise, largely owing to men in the same district working on the same or similar jobs having to get their instructions through different channels.   As a result of this, Plymouth suggests that

" steps should be immediately taken to ensure that, in future, all such instructions should be co-ordinated before being issued to any one organiser, particularly when there are other organisations catering for similar workers in the same town."

Pontypridd makes a similar point :—

" Much greater efficiency could be maintained if all the telegrams were sent to me as Secretary of the Strike Committee instead of to the several Trade Union branches."

The Sheffield report mentions at some length the difficulties which arose from lack of centralised authority locally, and its general conclusions on this point are :—

(a) That more power should have been vested in the local Trades Councils.

(b) That in all cases they should have been made responsible for interpreting the instructions of the General Council in accordance with the local position, and to decide between Unions in case of misunderstanding.

And among the many other indications of the desirability of local centralisation, Preston's comment may be quoted :—

" The need was being felt at the close of greater directional power being placed in the hands of the Central Strike Committee, rather than each branch having to obtain powers from its own Executive."

To a certain extent, the whole difficulty arises from the existing Trade Union structure.   But even given the existing multiplicity of Unions, there is no doubt that centralisation of instructions in the localities could be, and should be, arranged.   This means that the Council of Action should be the body to which all important communications should be addressed.   Whether such communications should emanate from the General Council, as suggested by Middlesbrough and other Councils, or from the separate Trade Union Executives, does not matter from the standpoint of local organisation, provided they come through the Council of Action, which would naturally settle doubtful points before, and not after, difficulties had arisen.   But there seems to be no reason why efficient and representative group sub-committees of the General Council should not issue the instructions, as in fact they were attempting to do by way of interpretation and co-ordination in the later stages.

Apart from supervision of the actual details of the stoppage, the Trades Councils were

" charged with the responsibility of organising the trade unionists in dispute in the most effective manner for the preservation of peace and order."

No other functions were laid down by the General Council, and if the instruction had been read literally by the Trades Councils their activities would have been limited to the formation of Defence Corps or other forms of Labour police to keep the Fascists or Government forces in order, combined with the organisation of meetings, entertainments and sports to keep the strikers in order. The nature of the emergency, however, was recognised by some Trades Councils from the start, and by others as the situation developed, and they undertook functions lying far beyond the literal meaning of the General Council's instructions. The detailed work is the subject of other chapters ; here it is only necessary to say that the Trades Councils, broadly speaking, extended their functions with a view to the mobilising and effective use of all the Labour forces in the area. The struggle was recognised as a class issue, and the functions necessary to secure victory for the working class were developed as fully as local circumstances would allow.

Chapter II.

HOW THE COUNCILS WORKED.

Centralisation and Control.

In examining the machinery through which the Councils acted, the point immediately arises of how far the various activities were really centralised, and how far they were carried out independently by the special committees which were set up. To a great extent, in practice, this depended on the frequency of the meetings of the Council of Action. At Macclesfield, for instance, in the early days there were two sessions daily, morning and afternoon ; at Wakefield an Executive appears to have been in more or less continuous session, with full meetings every other day ; at Middlesbrough there were full meetings every afternoon, and responsible delegates met every evening, while in its recommendations for the future Middlesbrough contemplates that the Central Strike Committee should remain in continuous session, adopting a three-shift system. There are indications in several of the reports that an Executive Committee or some of its members were in continuous attendance ; and it can safely be said that some such arrangement for continuous responsible supervision was felt necessary in most areas. At the same time, this is not a substitute for full meetings of the Council of Action or Central Strike Committee ; and it may be doubted whether Middlesbrough's suggestion of a three-shift continuous session is a good one.

Looking at the question from a practical point of view, the points to be considered are the necessity for *general contact* at frequent intervals, together with *special direction* of a continuous nature.   It is simply impossible for the full Council of Action to be in continuous session ;   its members must of necessity have responsibilities elsewhere, and their contact with the current work of their own particular organisation is essential to the proper functioning of the central body. Breaking up the full Council into three shifts perhaps gets over this difficulty, but it ceases then to be a full Council, and there would be a serious danger of different policies and even of rifts developing between the three sections.   The practical solution seems to be the one which was usually employed, of holding a full meeting every day, and the officers or other E.C. members being in attendance continuously.   Decisions on details—even on wider questions—can be settled by one or two officers, who naturally consult the groups specially concerned and in any case report their action to the full Council.

The same point arises in regard to the various committees set up by the Council.   Some responsible person must be in attendance continuously ;   in the work of every committee urgent questions arise.   At the same time, the committees should not become one-man shows, if only for the reason that under E.P.A. accidents may happen at any time to the one man ;   therefore the Council of Action should see that every committee meets at least once a day, and that understudies are provided.   The difficulty is that the work of the committees tends to become swamped with details, and the committee members are consulted as individuals rather than as a committee.   This should not be allowed to prevent formal meetings, which are essential to maintain general confidence and to be ready to deal with more serious points which would be bound to arise in a longer struggle.

Committees Set Up.

Some idea of the variety and comprehensiveness of the activities undertaken by the Councils is given by the following list of committees which are mentioned in the reports.   Where the work done seems to have been similar, the various names used have been grouped together, so that we get a clear picture of the ground covered.

> Distress, Relief, Class War Prisoners' Aid.
> Entertainments, Socials.
> Finance.
> Food, Prices.
> Meetings, Propaganda.
> Office Staff.
> Organisation.
> Permits.
> Pickets, Rota.
> Police, Defence Corps.
> Public Committees.
> Publicity, Information, Intelligence, Literature, Press, Publications.
> Research.
> Sports.
> Transport, Dispatch, Messengers, Lines of Communication.
> Vital Services.
> Women's.

Oxford, as might be expected, was responsible for the special Research Committee ; in other places such "research" (gathering and collating facts on the Mining Dispute and the Strike position) was carried out by the Publicity Committee in its spare time.

Many of the Councils appear to have functioned with only one or two Committees (Propaganda or Publicity was almost universal) ; while Bolton heads the list with nine Committees.   It should be noted that the special Group Committees which existed in some areas are not included in the list, as they were generally equivalent to a Group Strike Committee rather than a sub-committee of the Council of Action. In a few cases (Derby, Wakefield, for example) these group committees were an integral part of the Council's organisation ; but in others they seem to have been more or less independent.

The actual composition of the Committees (and of the staff which is under their direction) is partly a question of individuals ; but there is one point which should be brought out. In a few cases it appears that the principle of representatives of particular unions for jobs in their own line was applied. Thus the Transport Committees were often actually composed of Transport workers ; while the Office Staff committees and personnel were composed of members of the clerical unions. There is as yet no Union of Public Speakers ; but the Propaganda Committees were often composed of propaganda secretaries of the political organisations. This principle should be applied wherever possible for practical reasons, but it is essential that other members should be appointed, in order to ensure that the policy applied by the committee is the policy of the Council and not of any section.

The methods employed by the various committees naturally varied with their functions and conditions, and no general analysis is possible. But wherever details are given, it is clear that representatives of the committees gave regular reports to the Council of Action. No difficulty appears to have arisen between the Councils and any of their committees, and it can be said that in spite of the considerable initiative developed by many committees, the Councils, as a whole, were fully supporting their activities. The detailed work of the more important committees—propaganda, publicity, transport, defence—are dealt with in subsequent chapters ; the food and prices committees are discussed in connection with co-operative questions. The work of some of the other committees must, however, be briefly mentioned here.

PICKETS.

As a rule the ordinary strike pickets were organised by the particular unions concerned. In a few cases however the organisation of pickets was centralised under a committee of the Council ; and in others the separate picketing arrangements of the unions were supplemented by centrally-organised pickets for special points. In some mining areas, again, mass picketing of road transport is mentioned, but it is not clear whether this was spontaneous or centrally organised.

There are indications of a centralised picket organisation at Bolton, Leyton, Pontypridd, Stockton, and Wakefield ; while in its proposals for the future Middlesbrough intends—

" That a centralised picket organisation be formed, consisting of the Picket Masters from each trade, to be under the control of the Central Strike Committee, and from whose headquarters picketing shall be directed."

Bolton's centralised picket organisation was a great success, and mobilised 2,280 pickets in two days, which enabled the duties to be four hours on and twenty off. This wide distribution of duties is an absolute necessity, and on this ground alone centralisation would be justified. Every reader will probably know of cases where pickets have been regularly on for far too long periods ; and while Finsbury's report suggests " Hot refreshments for all-night pickets is desirable," the better plan, especially in a long struggle, is to have short spells of duty by distributing the work widely. The difficulty in getting pickets in some trades, again, makes it necessary to have a centralised force. The members of the picketing committee, if formed on the lines suggested by Middlesbrough, would naturally allocate their own men to their own places of work in the first place ; but a certain reserve force could be built up for use in general—and in particular in connection with road transport, where concerns are often small and scattered, and of course very badly organised. The experience of Methil suggests that such a picketing committee should work in conjunction with the Defence Committee where that existed.

DISTRESS.

Unfortunately, distress or relief committees must be an essential part of the local organisation. In the records of the Councils of Action, such Committees appear wherever the organisation was developed, and had to deal with exceptionally hard-hit families, with families of men arrested, and, after the strike, with victimised men and their dependants. To some extent the trade unionist can rely upon his Union, or individuals in the branch, to see him and his family through such difficult periods ; but not every Union can do enough, and it is therefore necessary to have a central distress organisation with special finance. In many areas the distress committees set up in the strike have continued to function by way of collecting funds for the miners.

To a considerable extent, the distress committees were able to arrange some temporary assistance, through the local Co-operative, for distress cases ; examples are given in Chapter V. Various ways of raising funds were also developed ; at Coventry, for example, all collections at meetings went to the distress fund, and at Tonbridge receipts from various entertainments were devoted to this fund.

Apart from the raising of funds and the administration of relief, the distress committees functioned occasionally by way of arranging bail for arrested workers, providing defence, and paying fines. The necessity for this work was not generally realised, and in all probability numbers of men have been imprisoned or fined who, with proper advice and assistance, would have easily got off more lightly. At the same time, the methods of the police in making arrests, and the whole policy of the arrests, were not exposed as they undoubtedly could have been if adequate assistance had been given to the men charged. Here again the various Unions gave such help as they could, but the strain on a central legal department was too great, apart from the inevitable difficulties of communication. Middlesbrough recommends :—

" That one or two persons be appointed who will undertake to arrange the defence of any member who may be arrested for strike activity."

This should certainly be done everywhere ; but also the legal points arising in an emergency should be circulated widely, so that arrested men know their legal rights, in particular that they can ask for a remand in order to get legal assistance. Another point is that a panel of thoroughly reputable persons who would stand bail should be prepared, and if possible agreed with the police at an early stage, so as to avoid delay in getting men out on bail.

ENTERTAINMENTS AND SPORTS.

The success of the Plymouth Sports Committee is historic ; at any rate the match between the strikers and police, when the Chief Constable's wife kicked off, was recorded widely in the press.   In numbers of other places sports and entertainments were also a great success, although there were also some failures to arouse enough interest.   As Castleford puts it, the aim generally was " to keep the minds of the men occupied " ;   but in practically every form of entertainment the general position must have been referred to, and the entertainment used not only to keep the men amused but also to keep up the strike morale.

The development of entertainments and sports during the Nine Days was not on the scale it should have been.   This, of course, was due to the utter inadequacy of existing workers' organisations in these fields.   The point cannot be discussed here, but it can be said that the building up of *workers'* sports and entertainments should be undertaken by every Trades Council which wishes to bring wider circles of workers under its influence, and that the existence of such institutions, even in times of " peace," would add a very powerful weapon to the armoury of organised labour.

Chapter III.

PROPAGANDA MEETINGS.

In the course of every industrial or political campaign constant and effective publicity is essential to success. It is not only a question of maintaining the morale of the fighters, but of drawing the attention both of fighters and of neutrals to the facts on which the conflict has arisen, and countering the enemy's propaganda. The importance of publicity in the circumstances of a General Strike cannot be over-estimated and it is to the credit of many of the Trades Councils that they realised this and took the necessary steps before the General Council showed any sign of activity in this matter.

The various forms of propaganda and publicity can be divided into the spoken word and the written word ; the first is dealt with in this chapter, and the next chapter covers the other forms—bulletins, leaflets, etc. As was noted in the chapter on organisation, by the end of the strike practically every Trades Council had its Propaganda or Publicity Committee ; the more active Councils set up such a Committee at their first meeting.

The organisation of public meetings, both open-air and indoor, is a normal activity of every local labour organisation. It was naturally a part of the activities of every Trades Council during the General Strike, and it is only in so far as any special points arose that the conduct of public meetings during the strike calls for special analysis or comment.

Open-Air Meetings.

In compact areas, such as those covered by the London Borough Trades Councils, the necessity to hold frequent meetings in various parts of the area made it necessary to draw in all available speakers, and to allocate certain pitches to be looked after by one or other of the affiliated organisations.   At the same time, general instructions were given to speakers by the Propaganda Committees ; speakers were supplied with local or central bulletins, and in some cases special speakers' notes were issued.   Oxford reports the setting up (through Ruskin College) of

" a research committee whose function was to gather and collate facts on the mining dispute and the strike position as it developed day by day, and supply the same to speakers."

But in most cases the speakers' notes were compiled from the bulletins of the T.U.C. by the Propaganda or Publicity Committees.

In areas where the Trades Council covered agricultural districts, or where the Trades Council was the only effective Labour organisation for many miles round, public meetings in the surrounding villages were organised, in addition to the meetings in the particular town where the Council operated.   Cambridge, Methil, Oxford and other Councils report sending out speakers over very wide areas, and thus helping to prevent any feeling of isolation and consequent loss of morale in districts which would otherwise have been completely at the mercy of the *British Gazette* and the B.B.C.

Methil Council reports that speakers were always sent out in threes—a miner, a railwayman, and a docker.   The principle was partially applied in other places, but it is one that future propaganda committees might make general—to have all platforms representative of the most important industrial groups in the area, drawing up a speakers' panel with that end in view rather than making it a mere list of individuals.

It is probable that a longer list could be compiled on the basis of industrial groups, and branches could be asked to supply speakers instead of only known individuals being approached.   The difficulty of collecting and moving speakers to the required points, which was an important matter in some areas, belongs to the question of transport, which is dealt with in Chapter VI.

In the early stages of the strike difficulties were anticipated from opposition at public meetings ;   but no such difficulties appear to have arisen, partly owing, no doubt, to the absorption of the Fascist groups on various activities for the Government, but mainly because the sympathy of the crowds was so definite that professional hecklers thought prudence the wiser course.   In some cases, as at Chatham, special pickets were sent to keep order at meetings, but there does not appear to have been any trouble even where no special arrangements were made.   The police attending meetings seem to have caused no trouble, and in many cases showed definite sympathy.

Bolton is unique in reporting :

" No open-air meetings held at all.   We kept our people off the streets as far as possible.   Result—not a single *Trade Unionist* arrested in Bolton."

This is no doubt a satisfactory result, but it is difficult to believe, on the experience of other areas, that the holding of open-air meetings would have had any different result.   Although Bolton had the use of two local cinemas for morning and afternoon meetings of strikers, besides distributing daily 4000 to 5000 copies of their local bulletin, the decision not to hold open-air meetings must have seriously restricted the number of persons influenced by their propaganda.   Freedom from arrests (even if it was really due to this) is dearly bought at the cost of limiting the use of such a powerful weapon in the struggle.

INDOOR PUBLIC MEETINGS.

In addition to the open-air meetings a certain number of indoor public meetings were held, often with " national " speakers. The main difficulty arising in this connection was the lack of available halls. The solution in most cases where no Labour hall existed was a personal appeal to the owners of suitable halls or theatres ; but two methods of meeting the difficulty are worth noting. The first was the use of Co-operative premises ; the second the use of the Town Halls or other halls controlled by a Local Authority. Stepney notes :—

" Fortunately we have control of the Guardians and Borough Council and all the latter's halls were placed at the disposal of the Council of Action. Meetings and concerts were arranged every night of the strike."

Wherever Labour was in control of the local government machinery considerable assistance was rendered to the Council of Action ; the development of this principle depends on the closer identification of Labour local authorities with the Trades Councils, a question which deserves more attention than it has received in the past.

The tremendous success of meetings and the un-expected size of meetings and demonstrations is a common feature of the reports. Audiences were easily gathered with little notice ; hall meetings had to be supplemented with overflow meetings. No failures are reported. In such a situation the workers are willing to stand any weather and for any length of time, in order to keep in touch with events and to demonstrate their solidarity. If any conclusion emerges from the reports, it is certainly that meetings and more meetings must be held, that frequent meetings play an important part in maintaining the morale of the workers and in developing the class consciousness on which success depends.

SPECIAL MEETINGS.

The holding of special meetings for strikers, or members of particular unions, was a fairly general feature, and does not call for special comment. Kettering, however, appears to have made a specially systematic use of such meetings, and it is a point which should be borne in mind. Kettering states that the object was to keep the strikers together, and it must undoubtedly have had considerable effect in maintaining the solidarity and general morale of the men on strike.

The only other type of special meeting reported (apart from entertainments, which are mentioned elsewhere) was the meeting for women. Kettering must be mentioned again in this connection ; while St. Pancras set up a special Women's Committee, one of whose functions was to organise meetings for women. These meetings appear to have been well attended, the main method of advertising being through the strike committees, contact thus being established with the strikers' wives—a most important factor in the struggle. Fortunately, the experience of Harwich seems to have been exceptional—

" The B.B.C. had a most demoralising effect on our women-folk, which reacted on their men."

Nevertheless, it is certainly essential to take special measures to keep up the morale of the women, and to give them a lively sense of solidarity with the men. To some extent this aim was carried out by many Councils through the Entertainments or Socials Committee, but it would seem, from the absence of any special mention of women in most of the reports, that as a rule no special efforts were made to extend propaganda to the wives of strikers and to women generally. Even in St. Pancras, where such efforts were made, they were only developed at a late stage in the strike, while all other activities had been provided for at an early stage.

Chapter IV.

LOCAL BULLETINS.

Of the 140 Councils which have sent in replies, 70, or one in two, appear to have issued local sheets for general distribution. It should be noted also that very many of the local bulletins were actually distributed in the areas of other Councils ; for example, the Liverpool bulletin was supplied in bulk to the Councils of Bootle, Ormskirk, etc., and similar arrangements are reported from many other centres. In addition to these, many other Councils issued special leaflets and a few copies of bulletins to be supplied to strike committee rooms, or duplicated the T.U.C. bulletin for strike committees or for posting in prominent places. The part played by these local bulletins was of the greatest importance ; in some cases up to 10,000 copies were issued daily, and everywhere the demand for them far exceeded the possible supply, whether they were distributed free or sold for ½d or 1d. Leigh reports that its bulletins were " eagerly sought after " ; Leyton says " distributed as soon as obtained." These are certainly cautious statements ; anyone who was concerned in the production of these bulletins will call to mind the queues of eager distributors waiting for supplies and the difficulty of getting the bulletins run off quickly enough to have another supply ready when the distributors returned with repeat orders.

The spontaneous appearance of these local bulletins was one of the most interesting features of the activity of the Councils. In a few cases the Trades Councils (or Labour Parties) were already issuing a regular local paper, printed or duplicated, and the issue of strike bulletins was comparatively easy ; but in most cases no such attempt had been made previously, and the necessary materials and personnel had to be got together under very difficult circumstances. The experience of members of the Communist Party in the production of factory papers proved of great use in many areas ; in others, again, the Independent Labour Party, the local Co-operative organisation or some Trade Union office provided the necessary material and qualified personnel.

The problems arising from the production of local bulletins are so numerous, and the various ways in which difficulties were solved of such vital importance for the future, that detailed examination of the reports on this subject is necessary ; while a few of the cartoons and some of the more humorous features are reproduced as features of special interest.

METHOD OF PRODUCTION.

In some of the towns a local Labour paper was in existence, and it would have seemed natural to continue it and even to transform it into a daily during the strike. The decision of the T.U.C. at the very beginning to stop all papers, whether on their own side or against them, was reversed in time to produce the *British Worker* ; but the result of the first decision was to create serious difficulties for the Councils, which turned at once to the printers' help in publicity work. Colchester reports having to duplicate its paper because—

" Printers out here would not allow us to print local Labour paper, though printed by small master-man (T.A.)."

Croydon managed however to get over the difficulty, and produced a bulletin printed by voluntary T.U.

labour, under the direction of the local Printing Trades Strike Committee. Leeds at first had to duplicate, but later was able to arrange for printing its bulletin (2 issues), and was finally used by the T.U.C. to print a local edition of the *British Worker* (1 issue only on the last day of the strike). Preston succeeded in producing a *Strike News*, printed by volunteer labour from the Typographical Society, plant being loaned for the purpose by a small local firm. Preston notes, however, that it was discouraged by the Publicity Department of the T.U.C. General Council—for what reason is not stated. Gateshead and other Councils were asked at a late stage by the General Council to print local editions of the *British Worker*, and some of these were successful in arranging the production after some hesitation on the part of the local branches of the printing unions.

In all other cases (so far as the reports go) the production of bulletins was carried out by means of typewriters and rotary duplicators, which generally had to be borrowed from some local organisation—Labour Party, Independent Labour Party, Communist Party, Co-operative, or Trade Union branch. Duplicating, of course, sets limits to the numbers of copies that can be produced, although in some cases up to 10,000 copies were issued daily, no doubt by the use of two or more machines and several stencils of the same page. The product is not so legible as a printed paper ; on the other hand cartoons are more easily introduced.

While, therefore, there seems to be every reason for utilising printing where the plant is available, duplicating is a useful auxiliary even from a technical standpoint, and in many cases will be the only possible method of production. It has the merit of being cheaper as far as the necessary equipment is concerned, and it is also of great use in the current work of the Trades Council, even apart from emergencies. The lessons to be drawn from the strike experience are that the Trades Councils should make permanent arrangements with the local printing unions on the one hand, and should also do everything possible to obtain an efficient typewriter and rotary duplicator. A list of machines in the possession of affiliated organisations (or individuals) should be kept ; and arrangements made with these, or with a friendly shop, to keep permanent stocks of paper, stencils and ink. Permanent arrangements on these lines would immensely simplify the work of the Council in an emergency, and would provide the necessary machinery for the various other activities of the Council.

STAFF AND CONTROL.

Most of the Councils which issued bulletins set up special committees to organise and control their production and distribution. These committees were appointed under various names :—Publicity and Editorial at Oxford, Press at St. Pancras, Publications and Publicity at Coventry, Publicity or Propaganda at other places. The exact functions and method of working of these committees does not appear from the reports, nor is it clear whether there was any attempt to control or censor the matter published. No disputes appear to have arisen in connection with what was put in the papers, and it can only be assumed that one or two members of the committee acted as responsible editors. The circumstances under which most of the papers were produced must have made any committee control impossible.

Although no internal difficulties are recorded, difficulties certainly arose through police action in connection with matter contained in the bulletins. Mexboro' reports that—

" The bulletins became a target for the police, therefore in future every care should be exercised in their publication."

Finsbury reports :—

"A local bulletin issued, and got fined £15 for same. . . . Police have all our sets."

And St. Pancras reports that its secretary was arrested and fined £10 in connection with a paragraph in the local bulletin. Many of the arrests of Communists were in connection with paragraphs appearing in local sheets issued by them.

In all the cases which are known to the writer, the prosecutions in connection with Trades Council bulletins arose out of paragraphs which were unnecessary, in the sense that they were merely news items and not declarations of policy or instructions. The remark made by Mexboro' that " every care should be exercised in their publication " seems to be fully justified ; while West Ham gives what seems to be a valid explanation of how offending paragraphs crept in generally—

" There was a tendency to collect all items of news, and in the absence of a supply of authentic news from the centre, this news so collected assumed undue importance."

To some extent, therefore, the question of matter appearing which was likely to cause difficulty with the police authorities depends on the supply of authentic news—a point which is dealt with under another heading. But there is a question of general policy involved. It is obvious that in certain circumstances the Councils of Action, in the interests of the workers, must print the truth even if it is unpalatable to the police authorities, *i.e.*, to the other side. The mere fact that a certain paragraph may lead to prosecution should not, from a working-class standpoint, be decisive against its publication.   But if a certain item is unimportant, in the sense that it has no bearing on the main question at issue, then the fact that its publication may lead to prosecution should at once condemn it to the waste-paper basket—or, to be more efficient, the fire.   And the responsible committee or editor should bear this in mind in relation to particular words as well as to paragraphs.

The problem of collecting, in addition to the editor, a qualified staff for the production of the bulletins seems to have presented no special difficulties.   Clerical help is generally available for local Labour organisations ;   apart from individuals, special help was forthcoming in many cases from the Railway Clerks' Association.   The suggestion that in future the clerical unions should be asked to supply any staff required is certainly a good one ;   where such branches exist it might be possible to spread the work over a number of people instead of piling it all on a few individuals. This is one of the many matters in which utilisation of Union machinery would considerably facilitate work, besides drawing in a number of new persons to activity in connection with the Trades Council.

NATURE OF CONTENTS.

The local bulletins which have been sent in with the replies to the questionnaire display a remarkable variety in the contents, make up, and general method of dealing with the news and announcements published.   Any attempt to describe them can only aim at selecting a few of the most typical features, and noting the different sources from which the matter was compiled.

The few printed bulletins which were issued do not call for special comment.   They were printed in ordinary newspaper form, and the contents were similar to those of the duplicated bulletins, except that they usually contained a larger proportion of matter directly taken from the *British Worker* and T.U.C. bulletins.

The form of the duplicated bulletins was usually one or more foolscap sheets, printed on one side only ; but where a large circulation was reached (and therefore supplies of paper were a problem) both sides were used. Most of the bulletins which have reached us have only a typed heading, and the contents are typed right across the page without any attempt at " display." These present the appearance of an ordinary duplicated circular, and although no doubt they served their purpose it is obvious that a little experience in the production of such papers would have added immensely to their psychological effect.

There were, however, many bulletins which were excellently produced, with a designed heading, with columns and clear breaks and sub-headings, and— the best feature of all—very topical cartoons. In the hope of creating local rivalries, we reproduce on the following page the first page of *The Workers' Chronicle* of May 7th, issued by the Newcastle Trades Council of Action, and on subsequent pages a number of cartoons from various other papers. These were, of course, drawn on ordinary paper and traced through the stencil with a sharp pencil or other instrument ; the designed headings were also produced in this way. The effect of cartoons in such a period of tension is immense, and as the technical production is so simple, publicity committees in the future might well make cartoons a regular feature. Local talent is generally available if an effort is made to find it ; and boldness of outline and imagination are more important than good technical drawing. Moreover, very little skill

EVENING EDITION   EVENING EDITION.

THE WORKERS' CHRONICLE.

ISSUED BY G.H. LARAMAN FOR

NEWCASTLE TRADES COUNCIL OF ACTION.

No. 4.   MAY 7th HALFPENNY.

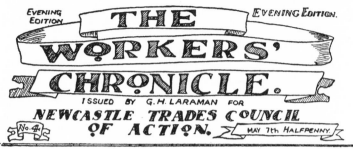

THE COUNCIL OF ACTION AND THE WITHDRAWAL OF PERMITS.

SIR KINGSLEY WOOD AND THE O.M.S. IN CHAOS.

The local Boss and Government press is making frantic efforts to keep up appearances, by printing statements in denial of the fact of Sir Kingsley Woods request to the Council of Action for joint working, we can only repeat our statement that such an approach was made

What is the meaning of these developments?, Firstly-it only means that the blackleg forces are failing the Government. Would Sir Kingsley have approached the Council of Action if he had not been in difficulties?

This is confirmed by the City Council's telegram of appeal to Baldwin. Secondly, the withdrawal wipes out the widespread abuse of permits by the more unscrupulous employers. Thirdly,- it places before the Civil Commissioner the question(bound to be reached sooner or later) of whether he will use soldiers (if they are available) and the military apparatus to the full in support of blacklegs, with the almost inevitable result of collisions with the workers on strike, or whether he will advise the Government that the attempt to break the strike has itself broken down

NO COMPROMISE WITH THE ENEMY.

A CORRECTION.

We reported yesterday that the General Bus workers were responsible for picketing activity in Chesten-le-Street, when we should have said the Northern Bus workers.

KEEP THE PICKETS AT WORK AND REPORT RESULTS

is required in " adapting " cartoons to new subjects, or even in compiling a cartoon from figures and drawings taken from some illustrated paper. In one of Low's usual articles in the *Star* some time ago he ingeniously worked out the necessary stock-in-trade of a political cartoonist, showing that a few typical figures were all that was required to produce the most varied cartoons. There is a good deal of truth in this, and with the help of a few such typical figures cut out of the press (especially the advertisement columns) even completely unskilled persons can produce striking cartoons.

As for the general arrangement of the bulletins, practically every paper began with some form of editorial explaining the general situation, nationally or locally, and calling attention to the Council's activities. This is followed by shorter paragraphs, often taken from the *British Worker*, the T.U.C. bulletins, or the *Sunday Worker* news service ; and local matters —reports, announcements, and news items—are distributed through the paper. Considerable prominence is given to the facts relating to the coal dispute, and the famous slogan, " Not a cent off the pay, not a second on the day " is frequently used. The warning not to believe the wireless or capitalist publications is a universal feature, and there are also many denials of particular statements by the B.B.C., the *British Gazette*, or other papers. Appeals for orderly conduct are also universal, and the T.U.C. statement that the issue was purely industrial is generally given and repeated in various forms. This, however, was combined with the clearest possible exposures of the Government's identity with the attack on the workers, and the fact that the workers as a class were fighting the capitalists as a class. The bulletins generally show an anxiety to avoid any " political " expression, coupled with an indefinite feeling that the issue was really political in the sense of being a struggle between the working class and the capitalist class.   A passage from the report sent in by Dartford Divisional Labour Party seems to sum up the general contradiction of ideas which is reflected in the editorial attitude of many of the bulletins :—

" On that issue (no wages reduction or increase in hours for the miners) the men were solid and their enthusiasm was white-heat.   But on the revolutionary issue they were cold.   (The English are not imaginative enough to produce revolutions).   After the third day of the strike, if you spoke about the coalowners the audience would listen with a polite indifference, but if you attacked the Government, or even mentioned the word, you had the audience with you and that with cheers and wild enthusiasm.   The issue was the T.U.C. and the Government—the miners and the owners were secondary to this issue."

Thus the conflict with the Government came to be the dominant issue in the editorial paragraphs, side by side with declarations that there was no political or constitutional issue.

On local matters, the same point appeared.   The Plymouth Strike Committee News Sheet of May 11th, for example, reporting the exclusion of Labour from an Emergency Committee set up by the Plymouth Town Council, mentions the reason given by the capitalist spokesman " that there were matters in connection with this situation which the Labour members of this Council ought not to know."   The comment ends—" IT IS CLASS WAR ! "

LOCAL REPORTS.

As already indicated, news of the position nationally was obtained mainly from the *British Worker*, the T.U.C. bulletins, or the *Sunday Worker* news service.

Some matter dealing with particular unions was obtained through circulars issued from the head office of the union.   Occasionally also a speaker or distributor of the *British Worker* would bring some special item which was passed on to the publicity committee. B.B.C. and *British Gazette* reports were mainly used to expose their lies ; the same is true of other capitalist papers.   In many cases the Councils arranged to have notes taken of the wireless " news " ; a few Councils installed wireless sets on the premises.

But the collection of local news presents greater difficulties.   Rumours were rife in those days, and considerable sifting had to be done.   Moreover, information on important points was not always easy to get.   Unfortunately, this question has not been dealt with in the replies from Trades Councils ; but the contents of the bulletins show that the local information must have been obtained from T.U. strike committees and from various sub-committees of the Council of Action, besides reports of local happenings which were probably supplied by individuals.   It is, however, noticeable that even the announcement of meetings was not a regular feature, while the official or semi-official statements about the position in particular unions cover only one or two of the many affiliated unions.   The impression is that the obtaining of reports was not done systematically—and this again was probably due partly to lack of organisation by the publicity committee and partly to the lack of response by particular strike committees to enquiries sent to them by the editor or publicity committee.   The obtaining of local material probably needs to be systematised in most areas.   Experience, especially in strike conditions, shows that general requests for information seldom produce continuous replies, and probably one member of the publicity committee should be definitely charged with the job of a reporter, visiting daily the secretaries of strike committees and other committees, and getting up-to-date and authentic information from each.   There are not many branch officials who realise the immense help which publicity can give them, and the appointment of a reporter would make it easier for the busy official to utilise the services of a local bulletin.   Such details as times of signing on, or place of signing on for particular groups (especially when, as often happened during the strike, the place had to be changed), should be regular features, as well as announcements of special union meetings or demonstrations and general messages to members.   This will not only .help the officials, but will also give the bulletin more interest for the rank-and-file.

Maintaining contact with strike committees has been referred to specially, but the same point holds good with regard to every other committee directing local activity.   Not only announcements but reports of work done should be regularly inserted, in order to arouse and maintain general interest and bring in active helpers in some sections of the work.

To sum up, the bulletins should be used not merely for conveying general news, but should play a real part in the organising work of the Council and of its component bodies.   Some of the local bulletins issued during the strike show that this general principle was realised ;   others give the impression of having been compiled from the T.U.C. bulletins or other general information, without any organic contact with the local movement.   This is a defect which can easily be remedied, and should be remedied in order to make the best use of the energy which is put into the production of the bulletins.

Brighter Bulletins.

We come now to another feature of the bulletins which undoubtedly helped to maintain their popularity and effectiveness—the humorous paragraphs and verses on current affairs. Their function is the same as that of cartoons—to " get it across " in a simple and telling form. Some of the bulletins evidently had the definite scheme of including some such matter in each issue. The *St. Pancras Bulletin*, for example, from its second issue (May 5th) ran a " Strikers' Alphabet," with three verses in each number. It was a very popular feature, and was copied by other London bulletins later :—

The Strikers' Alphabet.

(From the St. Pancras Bulletin, in instalments in Nos. 2-9, May 5th-10th, 1926).

A is for ALL, ALL OUT and ALL WIN,
And down with the blacklegs and scabs who stay in.
B is for Baldwin, the Bosses' Strong Man,
But he's welcome to dig all the coal that he can.
C is for Courage the workers have shown,
Class Conscious and Confident that they'll hold their own.
D is for DOPE that the Government spread—
Dishwash for Duncos and Dubbs—" nuf sed."
E is for Energy that will carry us through,
Everyone class-conscious, steadfast and true.
F is for Fight, our fight to the end,
For we're solid together, not an inch will we bend.
G is for Grab-all, the bosses, you know,
Greedy and grasping, one day they must go.
H is for Hardship, we all must endure ;
However, keep smiling, for Victory is sure.
I is for Interest, Profits and Rent
Into the pockets of the Indolent.
J is for Jix, the stirrer of strife,
Just waiting the chance to have your life.

K is for knife that is wielded by Jix,
Keep yourselves orderly and frustrate his tricks.
L is for London, where the T.U.C. meet,
Leading the workers the bosses to beat.
M is for Miners, for whose rights we must fight,
Maintaining the cause which we know to be right.
N is for Natsopa, who stopped dope from the Boss,
Narking Churchill and Jix, so Baldwin was cross.
O is for O.M.S., the scabbing patrol ;
Oh ! how they are working, digging the Coal ! !
P is for pickets on guard at the gates,
Pulling up blacklegs who scab on their mates.
Q is for Quandary the Government's in,
Quite certain now the workers will win.
R is for Railways that won't run alone,
Ready for workers to run as their own.
S is for Solidarity that is winning our fight ;
Stick well together, for Victory's in sight.
T is for Taximen joined in the fray,
Troubling the blacklegs to walk all the way.
U is for Unity, each one for all,
United we stand till the Government fall.
V is for Victory, of which we are sure,
Vanquishing the bosses for evermore.
W is for Workers' Wages and hours,
We are nearing the day when control is ours.
X is for eXit the whole boss class—
Xtra enjoyment for me and my lass.
Y is for Young Workers to whom fighting is new ;
Yes, Young, but determined to fight with you.
Z is for Zeal shown by the Vigilance Corps,
Zealous that workers aren't trapped by the law.

The " high hopes " of the versifiers (for each verse was generally a collective effort of the producing staff) were doomed to disappointment ; but the alphabet played its part.

Some bulletins contained verses quoted from standard works which were felt to have some bearing

on the situation ; but among the original verses the
following samples are worth reprinting :—

The Naughty Rail Clerks.

(From the Hendon Bulletin, May 10th).

(Dedicated to those offices which were deaf to the call and
with abject apologies to the 55,000 or so rail clerks
who were not so afflicted).

Ten naughty rail clerks said, " We'll stand by the men of
the mine,
But one of them slipped up *en route*, and then there were
but nine.
Nine naughty rail clerks made up their minds to wait,
One could not stand the pressure, and then there were but
eight.
Eight naughty rail clerks thought lack of work was Heaven,
But one black sheep felt out of place, and then there were
but seven.
Seven naughty rail clerks said " We're not afraid of Jix,"
One, on the way, read the E.P.A., and then there were but
six.
Six naughty rail clerks said, " Well, bless my heart alive,"
For looking round a second time, they found they were only
five.
Five naughty rail clerks, they had started half-a-score,
One became a Stationmaster, leaving only four.
Four naughty rail clerks, shaking at the knee,
One went out with a number book, and then there were
but three.
Three naughty rail clerks determined to be true,
But one did wag the old green flag, reducing them to two.
Two naughty rail clerks said, " Whatever's to be done,"
There was no sound, and looking round, one found he was
but one.
One naughty rail clerk for his mates did make atone,
He his strength did lend to the bitter end, although he was
alone.

—By the Poet Lor' 'e 'Aint.

PUFF, PUFF, PUFF, GOES THE ENGINE.

From *Paisley Strike Bulletin*, May 10th.

To Heaven by L.M.S.

Official Bulletin from 2 Hell-O S.B.
To all Stations.

(*From Bristol Central Strike Committee Bulletin,
May 11th, 1926*).

Early in the morning, per broadcast from London,
See the little puff-puffs all in a row,
D'Arcy on the engine, pulled a little lever,
Expansion of the boiler—Up We Go !

Railway Triolet.

(*From the Paisley Strike Bulletin, undated copy*).

" There's a train comin' in
At the station, my boys ;
Tho' there's only the yin
There's a train comin' in.
O ! the noise and the din
O ! the din and the noise ;
There's a train comin' in
At the station, my boys."

The humorous paragraphs were more numerous
than the verses, and selection is more difficult ; but
a few examples of the various subjects dealt with are
given below. The running of the railways came in
for special attention :—

The *Stockport Echo* yesterday :—" Flying Scotsman "
left this morning for London ; it will remain overnight at
York, and proceed in the morning. But they don't say
anything about the second night.
(*Stockport Strike Bulletin*, May 11th).

We understand that luncheon cars are to be put on
trains running between Westminster and Blackfriars.
(*Westminster Worker*, May 12th).

A train which left Manchester on Tuesday at 9.30 a.m. is reported to have arrived at Marylebone at 10.15 a.m. Friday.

(*St. Marylebone Bulletin*, May 8th).

The one train which passed the N.U.R. hut this morning carried no passengers, but had FOUR men on the engine. Loudly cheered by the men on strike.

(*Cheltenham Bulletin*, May 8th).

SOME DRIVERS !

And this is how they go, even when they *do run* :— It took three hours to travel by train to London last Friday, and three and a half hours to come back. The extra half-hour was added because the driver's trilby hat blew off, and the train stopped while the fireman went back to fetch it ! Better get some glue, says Bill Few, pomade doesn't seem to do !

Two level-crossing gates have been knocked down between Cambridge and Ely. The young gentlemen drivers mistook the gates for Cottenham hurdles, but their iron steeds failed to clear.

(*Cambridge Strike Bulletin*, No. 4, May 11th).

THINGS WE WOULD LIKE TO KNOW !

If, after the blackleg Amateur Signalman at Ribble Sidings had failed after trying for 45 minutes to get an engine into the Sidings and out again, the engine went to the shed disgusted ?

(*The Preston Strike News*, No. 3, May 10th).

But the O.M.S. provided a constant source of inspiration, both for cartoons (some of which are reproduced on other pages) and for paragraphs :—

Only 2 O.M.S. reported for pitwork. Upon finding no baths at pithead and that they had left tooth-brushes at home they declined, and returned to London by the "Normal Railway Service."

(*St. Pancras Bulletin*, No. 10, May 11th).

POP GOES THE WEASEL.

Yesterday (10th) a train from Earswick stopped at Haxby Road Crossing, where from 20 to 30 people were waiting. Two bright lads stepped off the engine, and came forward to open the gates, drawing revolvers to show that they really meant it, you know. When a locomotive turns awkward, all the really best people, you know, use a REVOLVER. Let an engine know that you understand its little way, what !

(*York Central Strike Committee Bulletin*, May 11).

STRICTLY UNOFFICIAL.

We understand that the L.G.O.C. has now completed arrangements for new working rules and uniform after the strike. Arising out of their experiences with the Noble Heroes who have been rallying to the Coy., the L.G.O.C. has decided as follows :—

1. Smoking will be compulsory at work.
2. Every driver and conductor will be accompanied by one Special, to hold his hand and count the money.
3. The following uniform will be issued to all grades :— One pair of plus fours, two pairs golf stockings (with tabs), one sports coat, green silk hanky, one pair kid gloves.
4. A bonus will be paid to all conductors who can wear a monocle and take fares without spilling it.

(*Hendon Bulletin*, May 12th).

Other paragraphs are of a more general character, some being decidedly not original, although given a topical setting which went home. Baldwin and Jix claimed honourable mention ; while one of the neatest special paragraphs was—

Notices posted on Cemetery Walls at Highgate and Finchley calling for Volunteers. We suggest that it should be picketed by Underground men.

(*St. Pancras Bulletin*, No. 11, May 12th).

Many of the reports of local incidents were written in humorous style, but are too long to quote here. These paragraphs and verses had an excellent effect in maintaining cheerfulness and morale, while they helped to drive home the more serious propaganda ; and although it is not a question of preparing jokes for the next general strike, the inclusion of such lighter material should be one of the definite aims of the publicity committees.

CHAPTER V.

ARRANGEMENTS WITH CO-OPERATIVE SOCIETIES.

IN the instructions issued by the General Council, no reference of any kind was made to the part to be played by the Co-operative Societies in the struggle ; they were not asked to help, nor were the Trades Councils asked to help them.   Discussion of why no special mention was made of the Co-operatives lies outside the scope of this book ; the general—but not universal—lack of connection between the Trade Union movement and the Co-operative Societies is, however, a fact which became only too obvious during the Nine Days.   While the General Council issued no instructions on this point to the Trades Councils, the Co-operative Wholesale Society issued a circular to Co-operative Societies in warning terms ;   and this was supplemented at a later stage by a further circular calling the attention of the Societies to the difficult position created by the General Council in refusing all permits and giving no exceptional treatment to the Co-operatives.   On a national scale, therefore, lack of sympathy was evident on both sides, and this was reflected in most districts, although in a few cases the local Society worked in close contact with the Council of Action.

Of some 140 Trades Councils reporting, 67 state that no arrangements of any kind were made with the local Co-operative Societies ;   but in a few of these cases, negotiations were on foot when the end came. In the districts where the local Co-operative Society was friendly, its chief method of assistance was by giving credit ; sometimes the Co-operative Society gave credit to its members up to the value of their usual weekly purchases, or up to some fixed sum ; more often credit vouchers were issued in cases of distress by the Council of Action or the Unions, and food was supplied by the Co-operative to be paid for later by the Council or the Unions.   Reports from 29 districts say that credit arrangements of this kind were made ; but several districts report that the Co-operative Societies declined to give any credit. This was the case in Doncaster, for example, although here facilities for the transport of foodstuffs were granted to the Co-operative Society only.   In five cases it is reported that the Co-operative Societies gave money (both as donations and loans) to the dis-tress funds, and in eight districts the Co-operative Societies provided meeting-rooms free for the use of Councils and Strike Committees.

One very important use of the Co-operative Societies was to fill in the gaps caused by delay on non-arrival of cheques from the Unions, and several districts report that the local societies advanced the strike pay when it would not otherwise have been forthcoming ; in other districts the societies acted merely as bankers for the Strike and Distress Committees.

In five districts it was arranged that directors or members of the committee of the local Co-operative Society should act on the Council of Action, Emergency Committee, or whatever the main organisation might be, either as full members or in an advisory capacity ; but it does not appear that any special plans were worked out.

The reports received are by no means all-inclusive, and some of them are, unfortunately, very vague ; Porth, for instance, states : " No arrangements of note were made with the Co-op. other than working with

From *St. Pancras Bulletin*, No. 4, May 6th, 2nd Edition.

them during that period." From the information received, the Coventry Co-operative Society seems to have been one of the most active during the struggle ; but even there the Council of Action made no definite arrangements with the Society. The Society, however, placed a car at the disposal of the Council of Action and stated that it would do anything possible to meet any demands of the Council. At a meeting of tradesmen, convened by the local Food Controller, the chairman of the Co-operative intimated that for at least 14 days there would be no increase in food prices at its stores. The other tradesmen were obliged to follow suit. The Co-operative also obtained coal, by permission of the Warwickshire Miners' Association, which they sold at 2/3 per cwt., thus preventing the other merchants from raising the price to 3/6, as had been intended. In spite, however, of these activities, the Council of Action apparently felt that closer relations and a more far-reaching plan of working should have been developed :—

" The important part of the Co-operative Societies cannot be too much emphasised, and everything possible should be done to fix up arrangements for the next round."

This view is shared by many of the other districts. It is recognised that the chief difficulty in the way is the conservatism and apathy of the leaders of the Co-operatives in many districts. Bolton, for instance, complains that its Co-operative Society is " largely a Conservative body and non-sympathetic," and similar statements occur in other reports.

But unfortunately it was not only on general grounds that hostile sentiment existed or arose. The trouble over permits affected practically every Cooperative Society. In some districts the Co-operatives were given permits by the Transport Unions to move and distribute food supplies, and here they mostly worked amicably with the Council. But in other districts, and at later stages, permits were withheld ; and the result was that the Co-operatives were more handicapped than the ordinary traders who received Government help in obtaining food supplies ; this naturally led to considerable local bitterness. The Colchester Strike Committee reports that relations became strained between it and the Co-operative Committee because permits, after a single issue, were refused ; and Edmonton reports that the action of the Transport and General Workers' Union in hampering the distribution of food supplies by the London Co-operative Society was much resented and made it impossible to make any arrangements with the latter. A similar situation developed in most other areas.

The reports under the heading of "Arrangements with Co-operatives " reveal what was perhaps the weakest section of the work done by the Councils of Action. To a great extent, as already indicated, the fault did not lie with the local organisations, which in some cases worked together harmoniously and usefully. But the general position is profoundly unsatisfactory, and the remedy is very largely in the hands of the Trades Councils. Croydon puts the solution in a nutshell :—

" There were no bad points locally—except that the workers haven't captured the Co-op. yet."

It is not merely that the Trades Councils should endeavour to make every trade unionist a member of the Co-operative Society ; this desirable object can probably only be attained when the Co-operative Society draws closer to the organised labour movement. The first step is to draw it closer—a step which it is in the power of most Trades Councils to carry out if they plan deliberately to do so. The Trades Council, as the co-ordinating body for the whole of the local movement in all its aspects, should put forward its candidates for co-operative committees and see that they get in, to carry out a programme of linking up the societies with the Trades Councils, and, above all, bringing the Co-operative machine into every industrial struggle, small or large.

The whole matter does not, however, end with the responsibility of the Trades Councils. The General Council's failure to develop its policy to meet the special needs of the Co-operatives, or to outline any plan for utilising them, was keenly felt by the Councils during the General Strike. Whatever the difficulties may be in the way of a national arrangement, they need not prevent the main question from being worked out. In a future emergency, it may not be only a question of supplying credit, but of supplying food itself. A parallel can be drawn with the Labour press : in a struggle between organised labour and organised capitalism, the *British Worker* and the local bulletins sprang into existence as necessary weapons in the fight, and it was generally recognised that the closing down of the Labour press had been a mistake. In the same way the Co-operatives must be considered and made into effective weapons for the workers, and must not be hampered in their working or treated in the same way as the capitalist food organisations.

CHAPTER VI.

TRANSPORT AND COMMUNICATIONS.

IN *Road Transport and the General Strike*, Mr. George Glasgow tells how the Government's detailed Emergency plans were elaborated months before the strike, and the country mapped out into districts and subdistricts for all purposes, but mainly for the purpose of maintaining communication with every part of the country.   On the workers' side nothing of the kind had been done, and the lack of preparation was felt most acutely in the sphere of communications.   The reports from the Trades Councils are eloquent on this point.   We find at the outset the problem arising of creating some regular channel of communication with the General Council ;   and then the need being felt of communication with neighbouring Councils of Action.   Efforts, and on the whole very successful efforts, were made by the Councils to establish communication ;   but examination of the reports shows the almost complete absence, even at the end, of any systematic plans covering the whole country.

The activities were, of course, almost entirely for the purpose of obtaining and giving news.   Transport in the sense of moving goods, apart from the distribution of the *British Worker*, mainly took the form, so far as the Councils of Action were concerned, of moving typewriters and duplicating machines. Preston, however, mentions arrangements for distributing coal to co-operators ;   while Plymouth and some other Councils helped the Co-operative Societies to obtain supplies.   But, generally speaking, the question of transporting goods did not arise ;   though it is clearly a question which would become important in a longer struggle, involving the organisation of food supplies for the whole working-class population.

In the development of a system of communications during the strike, the main requirements which had to be met were :—

(1) Contact with the General Council or other body which itself had such contact.
(2) Contact with neighbouring Councils.
(3) Contact within the area, with local Strike Committees, etc.

These contacts could only be maintained, first, by securing the necessary personnel and equipment ; and, secondly, by making an organised use of such personnel and equipment as were available.

PERSONNEL AND EQUIPMENT.

From the beginning of the strike practically every Council of Action was receiving offers of assistance from individual owners of motor cars, motor cycles, or ordinary cycles. In some cases, quite astonishing numbers are recorded. Bolton, for example, mentions having mobilised 57 motor bikes ; Colchester had the use of a car and many motor cycles ; Coventry had the offers of nine cars and sixty motor cycles; Mexboro' even complains of having had too many despatch riders ; while Methil had no fewer than three cars and 100 motor cycles. In all cases, as many ordinary cycles as were required were easily available. In addition to locally mobilised cars and cycles, the cars sent out by the General Council from London were often available for communication with London and other centres. On the whole, it does not appear that any lack of the means of communication was felt, although it may be only that the point is not specifically mentioned in the reports. So far as the need for cars and cycles was felt at all, it was generally a question of a temporary shortage owing to lack of organisation. On the other hand, and in spite of the excellent work done, the absence of a general scheme of communications led to considerable overlapping, while many areas were hardly in regular touch with the centre or surrounding districts.

If a general scheme had been in operation, therefore, it is possible that a shortage of personnel and machines would have been felt ; and consequently any scheme of communications should be accompanied by the preparation of lists of available persons and machines, so that they could be definitely mobilised from the outset of any future emergency.

In addition to machines, the question of supplies of petrol must be considered. There was, of course, no difficulty in obtaining supplies during the General Strike ; but if any shortage had existed, and if the Government had put into force any scheme of restriction or rationing, the position on the workers' side might have become very difficult. In this connection the Swindon report is suggestive ; there the Council arranged with the Co-operative Society to keep 300 gallons of petrol in hand for supply to dispatch riders.

Another interesting point is mentioned in the Coventry report : the readiness of qualified engineers to attend to cars or motor cycles if necessary. Special catering arrangements were made by some Councils for the use of dispatch riders.

ESTABLISHING LINES OF COMMUNICATION.

Although the question of available personnel and material is one that deserves most careful attention and preparatory work, the more fundamental question is the preparation of plans for the economical and effective use of whatever machinery is available. Viewing the position that arose as a whole, it can be said that no plans existed at the beginning of the strike, and although here and there, as particular needs were felt, some very effective work was done, it was seldom more than a series of individual efforts, without systematic guidance and control.

Owing to delays in receiving instructions in various districts, and to the anxiety to get authentic information from the centre, the Councils of Action in various parts of the country began to send dispatch riders to the General Council as early as Tuesday, May 4, and throughout the strike energetic Councils of Action maintained a regular or occasional service to Eccleston Square. At the same time the General Council itself gradually developed an occasional service to the provinces. The systematisation of communications with the centre is obviously a problem which can only be handled by the centre, but equally obviously it is impossible to set up any comprehensive system without a large measure of decentralisation.

The beginnings of such a comprehensive system were actually established. From the outset certain important towns had established communications with surrounding areas ; to take only a few examples, Bath was in touch with local organisations within a thirty mile radius ; Bolton developed lines of communication practically throughout Lancashire ; Middlesbrough was in connection with a number of important centres ; Wolverhampton established communications with Stafford, Manchester, Shrewsbury, etc. When the General Council began to systematise the distribution of its bulletins and of the *British Worker*, these active centres were asked to undertake to cover specific areas, distributing material from the centre and collecting reports for forwarding to the General Council. Coventry, for example, reports that it

" was made a centre by the General Council for the distribution of propaganda, etc., to Rugby, Warwick, Leamington, Nuneaton, Hinckley and Redworth. Also, at the outset of the dispute, Coventry took over from Nuneaton some half-dozen colliery and railway villages, and also found it necessary to cover a number of other villages which had not been specifically allotted to it."

Cambridge organised the distribution of 15,000 to 20,000 copies of the *British Worker* for East Anglia, excluding Norwich.

But in spite of these and other similar examples, the general impression given by the reports is that there was no very clear demarcation of areas or regular and comprehensive service. Coventry, for instance, which appears to have been among the most energetic Councils in tackling this problem, notes that—

" a timed service was gradually being worked out which would have linked up the whole of the district."

Probably West Ham's remark is true of the whole country—

" The general question of lines of communication only began to be settled satisfactorily towards the close of the strike."

DISTRIBUTING POINTS.

What should be the distributing points in a comprehensive and decentralised scheme ? This question is closely connected with the general question of the grouping organisation of Trades Councils—the Federations of Trades Councils, a matter which is dealt with in Chapter VIII. But certain points made in the reports in connection with lines of communication may be discussed here.

The Dartford Divisional Trades Council, approaching the question as a central body uniting a half-dozen local Trades Councils, thinks that the link should be an organisation in every Parliamentary division :—

" This would relieve the central body of a tremendous amount of work. The central body would maintain contact with the Divisional body, and the Divisional body contact with the area Council of Action or the local Trades Council."

But this, however necessary in a chain of communications, seems still to expect too much of the central body ; and in all probability a more practicable immediate link with the central body would be a Federation covering a far wider area than the Parliamentary Division. This is the proposal put forward by the Tees-side Federation ; and the London Trades Council intended, but did not realise, centralisation of all London Councils. The conditions existing at the time of the General Strike, however, made any such centralisation of communications impossible ; neither the London Trades Council nor the Federations had any organisation that could have coped with the work. Therefore the allocation of areas to particular active Councils, without any comprehensive scheme, was probably unavoidable ; but this does not mean that the method was good, and it is essential that a better system should be worked out, which will both cover all the ground and limit the duties put upon any particular Council.

Contact with neighbouring Councils was felt to be necessary almost everywhere, and the instances quoted above show how far afield lines of communication went from some of the Councils. But here again the lack of system was evident. Paddington notes the—

" lack of any kind of rules, etc., to link up with neighbouring Councils for uniformity of action."

Even within the London area any attempt at a systematic exchange of information between different
Councils only began towards the end of the strike.
News of course filtered through by means of individuals,
and the London bulletins contain brief messages from
neighbouring Councils ; but it was generally left to
chance whether any such messages came through.

The problem of linking up with other surrounding
Councils is, however, like the links with the General
Council, a problem of the general district organisation
of Trades Councils, and as such is dependent on the
points dealt with in Chapter VIII.

The question of establishing regular lines of communication within the area of a particular Council is
one which comes entirely within the scope of the local
organisation ; even in this there is evidence of lack of
system, although some Councils seem to have developed
a good organisation, such as Porth, which reports—

".the linking up of every Strike Committee and the exchanging of news by a courier system, which was very
successful."

It is true that such exchange of news within an area
should take place in the daily meetings of the Council
of Action ; but there is the distribution of the local
bulletin, the transmission of urgent messages from the
General Council, etc.   Reference has already been
made, in Chapter IV., to the necessity of a regular
connection with the separate Strike Committees for
the sake of the local bulletin.   It is obvious that a
committee which is producing the bulletin, or which is
carrying on any other special work, should not be
expected to arrange its own links.   All dispatch riding
and messenger work should be arranged, as was done

in Southall Norwood, through one centre to avoid overlapping—and also to avoid the absence of communications owing to the particular committee concerned having no messenger at its disposal. The Stockport report deals with this question in some detail ; the Transport Sub-Committee there consisted of members of the Transport Unions, and was to provide messengers for the rota committees, as well as dispatch-riders for more extensive work.

To sum up, the whole question of transport, even in the limited sense of maintaining lines of communication and distribution for bulletins, etc., seems to require far more systematic treatment than it received during the strike ; but as far as the main links with the centre are concerned, the question is bound up with the more general question of providing some regional organisation capable of linking up, directly or indirectly, with every Trades Council or Strike Committee in the region. Within any particular area, the transport and dispatch organisation should be centralised under a special committee, in order that comprehensive services can be worked out and the most efficient use made of such men and machines as are available.

CHAPTER VII.

ARRESTS AND WORKERS' DEFENCE.

IN the section of Chapter I. dealing with Distress Committees, various points connected with legal and financial aid for arrested persons have been mentioned. But the problems facing the Councils of Action went much deeper than aid for arrested persons. The arrests themselves were in part based on political actions by the victims : as the reports show the members of the Communist Party were especially singled out for arrests under this heading. But the attack of the capitalist State machine was not confined to arrests of speakers or writers (or distributors) of " sedition."

From the time when the Fascist and O.M.S. organisations came into existence in this country, it became clear that the capitalist class was preparing a huge strike-breaking machine, including the use of terrorism, and that, as in Belgium, it would be necessary to form a Labour force which would be in a position to defend the workers against the methods of Italian fascism. The co-ordination of the Fascist and O.M.S. forces with the police, which had been carefully organised since the summer of 1925, was actually carried out at the beginning of the strike ; and some of the Councils of Action realised from the start the type of terrorism which would be attempted.

The position in various areas actually became extremely serious at an early stage in the strike ; intimidation of properly authorised pickets and police charges in crowded streets took place ; strikers were batoned and arrested ; and although the overwhelming sympathy of the audiences at public meetings apparently frightened off any intended attacks, there were good grounds at the beginning to anticipate police and other interference. In such circumstances the formation of a workers' police, under one name or another, became a necessity in many areas, while in others it was felt that preparations should be made for the sharpening of the conflict which it seemed the Government was determined to bring about.

Such bodies of workers' police, or Workers' Defence Corps, as they were usually called, are specifically mentioned in the reports of Aldershot, Chatham, Colchester, Croydon, Denny and Dunipace, Methil, St. Pancras, Selby, Sowerby Bridge, and Willesden. At Aldershot the force was only being organised at the end; at Chatham and Colchester the force took the form of special pickets for meetings; Denny and Dunipace and St. Pancras seem to have organised the force, but not used it. At Sowerby Bridge—

"A few men appointed to assist in maintaining peace in the streets and highways—a huge success."

At Croydon, Methil, and Willesden fairly large forces were developed. At Methil a corps, which had been organised with 150 men, was raised to a strength of 700 as a definite reply to police charges on pickets, and was used for regular patrol work, the result being—

" There was no further interference by the police with pickets."

No definite conflicts between the defence corps and police appear to have taken place, in some cases, as at Methil, evidently because the corps was strong enough to deal with aggressive action; in others, as at Selby, because the police actually recognised the assistance given by the corps in preventing any trouble arising.

From Newcastle *Workers' Chronicle*, No. 11, May 11th, 1st Edition.

The position at Lincoln was of special interest. There—

" The police asked us to supply the whole of the Special Constables—which we did."

This is certainly an interesting example of the existence of good terms with the police which is reported from many other towns ; but the position created at Lincoln was not without its dangers. If, for example, military or mounted police had been sent to that district against the wishes of the local authorities, and had taken provocative action, the position of workers sworn in as special constables might have become very difficult. At the same time, providing they remained under the orders of the Council of Action, their position, though difficult, might have proved of immense value to the workers. In spite of the many examples of police aggression of the type that occurred at Poplar, the examples of friendly relations with the police are also numerous. The football match with the police at Plymouth has already been mentioned, and many other reports mention general friendliness. In some cases general friendliness was supplemented by overt acts ; Ilkeston hints at these in the sentence—

" Police very good and sooner assisted than interfered with us."

And Swindon is more precise—

" When our autocratic Mayor sent two tramcars on the streets the police allowed our strike leaders to take charge of the situation."

The friendliness with the local police was a most important factor ; often they were not merely friendly in the sense of avoiding provocative action, but definitely sympathetic with the object of the strike. Most of the cases of provocative action by police were actually due to imported police acting in conjunction with specials of the plus-four type, who had had their mental training in the Fascisti, O.M.S., or other similar organisation.

In *General Strikes and Road Transport*, Mr. George Glasgow gives the official attitude :—

" The susceptibilities of special constables were humoured in an original manner. It was thought that a special constable, recruited from a given village, might feel some compunction about summarily arresting his best friend for seditious talk on the village green. Mobile fleets of special constables were therefore recruited far away from the possible danger zones, and they dashed through those zones as strangers."

Put in blunter language, the Government could not trust the " loyalty " of the forces who knew the inhabitants and the working conditions in the area ; and therefore where police attacks were to be employed, men from distant areas were drafted in, and probably carefully fed with anti-strike propaganda before being used. These methods account for the contrast between the friendliness of the local police in so many cases, and the indiscriminate attacks made in other places by imported police, or where Fascist sections of specials were given a free hand.

We cannot deal in detail with the particular cases of arrests, the nature of the " evidence," or the vindictive sentences imposed. One or two examples from the reports and local bulletins may, however, be quoted. At Accrington a small boy was arrested for throwing orange peel at a charabanc ; the report unfortunately does not say whether this act was " seditious " or " disaffecting." At Bolton ten lads received up to three months' sentences for drawing the draw-pin of a coal cart ; and at Farnworth a man was sent to gaol for a month for tearing down a Government poster. The trams were used in many areas as a means of collecting a few prisoners; they were run out from the depots and the inevitable reception was met by police charges and numbers of arrests. In some cases the police charges and the arrests took place without the formality of getting the cars out. At Brighton, police charges near the tram depot resulted in 22 arrests and sentences of from one to six months; but in spite of this the motion to form a Defence Corps was rejected by the Council of Action.

To sum up the reports on the subject of arrests and workers' defence, it can be said that in the majority of the areas reporting the necessity for special defensive measures did not arise, very largely owing to the friendliness of the local police and the absence of Fascist elements in the local administration or of imported police.   At the same time, in a few areas the necessity of a Workers' Defence Corps was felt, and at least the nucleus of a corps established; while in many other areas provocative action and arrests took place on a scale which would probably have made a defence corps essential had the strike been of longer duration.

In a few cases the nucleus of a Workers' Defence Corps is being maintained, but there is no indication of a widely organised scheme such as the Trade Unions in Belgium developed in response to the growth of Fascism there a few months before our General Strike.

CHAPTER VIII.

LINKS WITH THE GENERAL COUNCIL.

IN its preparation for the General Strike, the Government divided England and Wales into ten Divisions and Scotland into five districts for the purpose of co-ordinating the work in the innumerable smaller areas within each district. No attempt was made on the workers' side to create any new co-ordinating bodies in wide districts for the conduct of the strike, nor was any use made of the machinery—admittedly very rudimentary—which already existed in the Federations of Trades Councils.

The essential point has already been raised in an earlier chapter in connection with transport problems. Direct administration by one central body of all the local organisations is a physical impossibility, especially during a crisis. When, in addition to the one central body—the General Council—there are also a large number of other central bodies—the Trade Union head offices—the problem becomes more complicated. And when these central bodies are communicating not only with the one central body in the localities—the Trades Councils—but also with innumerable joint strike committees and branches, chaos is unavoidable. The necessity of some form of district organisation is therefore evident, and appears from many of the reports to have been acutely felt during the strike.

Before dealing with the reports, however, reference must be made to the resolution on Federations which was adopted by the National Conference of Trades Councils in March, 1926. The resolution was :—

" That this Conference approves the following scheme for the federation of Trades Councils, and authorises the Committee to make arrangements for the calling, where necessary, of meetings of Councils in the given areas with a view to establishing the new Federations."

COUNTIES.	Number of Trades Councils.	COUNTIES.	Number of Trades Councils.
1. Northumberland, ...	5	7. Cambridgeshire,	3
Durham, ...	13	Norfolk, ...	6
Cumberland, ...	4	Suffolk, ...	7
2. Westmoreland, ...	2	8. Bedfordshire,	5
Lancashire, ...	65	Essex, ...	12
Cheshire, ...	13	Hertfordshire,	7
North Wales and Isle		Buckinghamshire,	7
of Man, ...	2	Oxfordshire, ...	1
		Berkshire, ...	4
3. Yorkshire, ...	48		
		9. Surrey, ...	15
4. Derbyshire, ...	7	Sussex, ...	7
Nottinghamshire, ...	7	Kent, ...	21
Leicestershire, ...	5	Hampshire, ...	10
Lincolnshire, ...	8	Middlesex, ...	6
Northamptonshire, ...	8		
		10. London, ...	52
5. Staffordshire, ...	18		
Shropshire, ...	4	11. Wiltshire, ...	4
Herefordshire, ...	2	Gloucestershire,	6
Warwickshire, ...	8	Somersetshire,	10
Worcestershire, ...	6	Dorset, ...	4
		Devonshire, ...	9
6. South Wales and Mon-		Cornwall, ...	4
mouthshire, ...	39		

The general objects of such a scheme of federation are stated in the General Council's report to the Bournemouth Congress, as under :—

" This resolution contains a skeleton scheme for all-inclusive federation. At the present time there is a large number of Trades Councils working entirely on their own. They are consequently unaware of general policy in sur-rounding areas, and are not receiving the assistance which could be rendered to them if all Trades Councils in a given area are to be grouped in a federation in order that policy may be co-ordinated and the weaker Councils advised and assisted in organisation. Certain district federations of Trades Councils are already in existence, and the position is being examined in order to ascertain how far these organisations can function in the new scheme. When this examination is completed and several small but important details have been reviewed, meetings will be called in each of the eleven areas for the establishment of the final scheme."

In a time of emergency all the reasons for such Federations are especially convincing, while the special need arises of some authoritative body which is able to act as an intermediate authority between the separate Trades Councils and the General Council.

To a certain extent, as was pointed out in connection with transport, intermediate authorities were set up in the course of the strike, largely on their own initiative. The Council of Action in many large centres acted as a link between the General Council and the neighbouring small towns and villages, distributing instructions and literature, and obtaining reports for transmission to the General Council. The arrangement, however, appears to have been rather one-sided ; the large towns helped the small towns and villages, but got no help from them, and there was no general attempt to bring representatives of these smaller places into organised contact with the Council of Action in the large centre. The report from the Hampshire and Isle of Wight Federation is an extreme case ; there " owing to the enormous area covered . . . no organised work was undertaken," the Secretary himself being used by the General Council to maintain communication between London and South Wales. This complete abandonment of the work of district co-ordination was not universal, but such reports as cover this point serve to indicate that up to the end of the strike very little was achieved, except in the sphere of communications.

In the London area, for example, with its 52 Trades Councils under the Federations scheme, a decision was taken as early as April 29 by the co-ordinating London Trades Council to summon a conference of delegates from the subordinate Councils together with representatives of the District Committees of the Unions involved. But actually no such conference took place ; the London Joint Strike Committee was formed of the Executive of the London Trades Council and representatives of the Unions, but at most a rudimentary messenger service was maintained with the 52 subordinate Trades Councils, which were constantly feeling the lack of organic connection among themselves.

A somewhat similar position occurred in Northumberland and Durham. The actual Joint Strike Committee was composed in the main of district representatives of the Unions ; a conference of Trades Councils was actually held on May 8, but the Joint Strike Committee apparently made it clear that this Conference had no powers, and no form of federating organisation was set up.

The Methil and District Trades and Labour Council constituted itself into a Council of Action for East Fife, which was apparently built up on a semi-federal basis, with representatives of local strike committees, etc., in different parts of the area covered ; and the Merseyside Council of Action, with two delegates from each of the Trades Councils around Liverpool, seems to have functioned as a federal body, but covering a relatively small area. Dartford Divisional Labour Party, with its six affiliated Trades Councils, is another instance of the same type, and probably many other examples occurred which are not covered by the reports.

But the fact remains that there was no general attempt to establish any comprehensive system of intermediate links between the General Council and the individual Trades Councils, and the question arises as to the best form of such an intermediate organisation, the necessity of which was felt during the strike—and would have been increasingly felt had the strike continued and the general position become more acute. Intermediate organisation based on district representatives of trade unions, such as existed in London and Northumberland and Durham, does not meet the need for organised contact with the individual Trades Councils. On the other hand, the existing Federations of Trades Councils do not meet the need—in view of the existing structure of Trade Unionism—for organised contact with the Trade Union machine. The obvious solution is the combination of these two groups to form a single District Council of Action, just as the local Councils of Action combined the Trades Council with the local Strike Committees.

The following scheme adopted, on the basis of the strike experience, by the Tees Side Federation of Trades Councils, is of great interest in this connection :

Tees Side Federation.

A Special Meeting of the Federation was held in Middlesbrough on September 25th, 1926, to consider a report compiled by the Secretary (from information received from Strike Committees, etc.) on the necessary action to be taken by the Tees Side Federation in the event of any future General Strike. The following were the recommendations agreed to by the meeting :—

1.—That in the event of any future National Crisis a Special Meeting of the Federation be called at once, by telegram if necessary, for the purpose of discussing the situation, Chairman and Secretaries of all Trades Councils and District Committees of Joint Branch Committees to be invited to attend the meeting.

2.—That a District Strike Committee be appointed at this meeting for the purpose of co-ordinating the activities of each Local Central Strike Committee.

3.—That this District Committee remain in continuous session by adopting a Rota System.

4.—That all officials be elected at this meeting and that sub-committees be set up to deal with (a) Despatches, and (b) Publicity.

5.—That a system of Dispatch Riders be set up for the purpose of keeping in touch with all Central Strike Committees and with the National Controlling Body.

6.—That the Publicity Committee shall issue a daily Strike Bulletin which shall be distributed throughout the area through the agency of the various Central Strike Committees.

7.—That the District Strike Committee shall be the central authority to control such National Crisis locally, and it shall issue such rules and regulations as it may think fit to control same.

8.—That all Central Strike Committees in this area shall be requested to send in a daily report of strike activities, number of people out, and other information, that is likely to be of service to the District Strike Committee. This information to be forwarded to all Central Strike Committees and/or published in the Bulletin at the discretion of the District Strike Committee.

9.—That the T.U.C. or other National Authority responsible for the T.U. side of the emergency shall be requested to forward all instructions direct to the District Strike Committee, who shall at once cause same to be distributed to all Central and Branch Strike Committees under its jurisdiction.

10.—That the cost of carrying on these activities shall be borne by the constituent bodies on a pro-rata basis.

It is not certain, however, that this scheme meets all requirements even on the organisation side.   The special character of the best local Councils of Action was their comprehensiveness, the fact that they united every phase of the movement.   If we think of the tasks which such a District Council of Action might be called upon to perform, it seems obvious, for example, that direct representation of the Co-operative Societies would be essential.   The London Trades Council (in essence a Federation) makes it clear that its aim is to include Co-operative representation, and— although there are many difficulties to be over-come—the whole experience of the strike suggests that any Federating body should include Co-operative representatives.   There are also advantages to be gained by the inclusion of the district political organisations, the women's organisations, and Labour Local Authorities.   On the whole, therefore, although there is not sufficient experience of the working of such a District Council of Action to justify any detailed suggestions, it can be said that the aim should be to establish an all-in organisation on a district basis, though the details might vary considerably from one district to another.

With regard to the functions of these District Councils of Action, the scheme of the Tees Side Federation leaves little room for criticism.   It depends, of course, on the General Council of the T.U.C. and the Trade Union Executives agreeing to " recognise " the District Councils of Action and working through them ; but after the experiences of the General Strike the devolution of authority combined with co-ordination over wide areas seem to be essential features of any plans for the future.

The final question to be considered is whether the emergency district organisation on the lines indicated should be purely an emergency organisation, or whether it should be the model for the permanent organisation

of the Trades Council Federations.   In approaching
this question, the existing weakness of the Federations
must be taken into account.   There are immense
difficulties in the way of any attempt to strengthen
them—the absorption of active individuals in local
work, difficulties of time, transport, etc. ; and although
the London Trades Council may develop an active
and all-in federal body with comparative ease, the
problem will be far more formidable in other areas.
Nevertheless, the reasons which justify the all-in local
Trades Council hold with equal or greater force for the
District organisation.   Such problems as the organisation of agricultural workers, for example, require
the co-ordinated efforts over a wide area of Trades
Councils, Trade Union District Committees, Co-operative Societies, political organisations and Labour local
authorities, etc.   The same can be said of every
industrial, co-operative, or political campaign.   For
these reasons, it seems essential that the Trades Council
Federations should aim at the widest possible basis
of organisation.   Moreover, on this wide basis it may
be possible to overcome the financial difficulty which
is at the root of all other difficulties in the development
of the Federations.   Premises and full-time officers
are essential ;   and the local Trades Councils cannot
possibly provide these without assistance from central
bodies.   But the creation of efficient district co-
ordinating bodies would be well worth while to the
national organisations concerned, and would be of great
help in all campaigns and other activities undertaken
by the General Council.

CHAPTER IX.

PROBLEMS FACING THE TRADES COUNCILS.

IN the preceding chapters the activities of the Trades Councils during the General Strike have been reviewed, and an attempt has been made to indicate, on the basis of their experience in May, 1926, the forms of organisation and preparatory work which would enable the Trades Councils to act more systematically and effectively in any future emergency. But the Trades Councils cannot confine their activities to times of emergency. The struggle against capitalism is continuous, and schemes for emergency action, however well devised, will inevitably break down when the crisis comes unless the necessary conditions for successful working have been created during the period of relative peace. It is the aim of this chapter to summarise briefly what those necessary conditions are, and how they can be brought into being.

The objects and methods of Trades Council work have been laid down in some detail in resolutions adopted by the Annual Conferences of Trades Councils held under the auspices of the Trades Union Congress General Council in 1925 and 1926. The resolutions which are relevant to the subject under discussion are printed below :—

RESOLUTIONS ADOPTED BY THE FIRST NATIONAL CONFER-
ENCE OF TRADES COUNCILS, FEBRUARY, 1925.

1. " That this Conference calls for greater unity in the trade union movement, and urges upon all members of trade unions the necessity of working assiduously towards obtaining 100 per cent. organisation and securing

co-ordination of effort between all unions—local, national and international, in conformity with national decisions."

2. " That this Conference recognises the desirability of securing to the workers in time of stress the best possible means of existence, and to this end calls upon all trade unionists to support and participate in co-operative undertakings, and to consider ways and means of providing food, shelter, etc., for those who are on strike or locked out, and urges all co-operative managements to insist that all their employees are members of their appropriate trade unions."

3. " That this Conference, realising the use which is being made by employers of welfare schemes and the provision of playing fields for their workers, urges upon the Trades Councils the necessity for their organising sports and entertainments for the workers in conjunction with the unions."

RESOLUTIONS ADOPTED BY THE SECOND NATIONAL CONFERENCE OF TRADES COUNCILS, MARCH, 1926.

4. " That this Conference urges all Trades Councils to adopt the Model Rules approved by the General Council, and that in the case of a Trades Council and Labour Party, the rules be adopted as governing the Industrial Committee of that body.   Further, in the case of Trades Councils, which consider as one body matters both of an industrial and of a political nature, this Conference urges that provision be made for an Industrial Committee which shall discuss and decide all questions of a purely industrial character, and be governed by the Model Rules."

5. " That this Conference recommends each Trades Council should supply to the Trades Councils' Joint Consultative Committee a list of the branches of Unions not affiliated, with a view to the Executives of the Unions being requested again to use their influence to secure, through Trades Councils, the linking up in localities of the whole Trade Union membership."

6. " That this Conference calls upon Trades Councils throughout the country forthwith to engage in organising campaigns in their respective districts, and for the purposes of these campaigns recommends :—

(a) That the services be sought of District and National Organisers of Unions catering for workers in the district.

(b) That a system of personal canvass similar to that employed during elections be adopted.

(c) That steps be taken, by means of paragraph (b) and by delegates raising the question at branch meetings, to urge upon trade unionists the importance of exerting influence upon their children to become Associates or Juvenile members of a Trade Union as soon as they start work, and to apply for full membership upon reaching the age of 16 years.

(d) That existing Trade Unionists be urged to develop and strengthen organisation inside the workshops.

(e) That the General Council be requested to provide necessary and suitable literature for assistance in these campaigns.

(f) That the General Council be requested to recommend Trade Unions which do not provide for Juvenile Associates to consider the matter with a view to making provision for young workers under the age of 16."

Structure of the Trades Councils.

In the model rules and constitution for Trades Councils, adopted by the General Council and approved in the resolution of the 1926 Conference of Trades Councils, the essential points are :—

Par. 3.—The Council shall consist of Trade Unions or branches of Trade Unions, whose places of meeting are within the area covered by the Council.

After the experience of the General Strike, it is difficult to regard this limited basis as satisfactory. It seems essential to the future of the movement that there should be one co-ordinating body in each locality, which would direct and be the expression of the whole of the Labour movement.   Because of the fact that the trade unions are the basis of the movement, the only body that can fulfil such a function is the Trades Council or joint Trades and Labour Council.   Similarly, where the local Labour Party is at present the only co-ordinating body, it is essential that it should function as a Trades and Labour Council, linking up the industrial movement in the area and giving full expression to the industrial as well as the political needs of the workers.   The Council of Action in its most comprehensive form is the most suitable model, embracing representatives of the workers' economic and political organisations, of the Co-operative Societies, of Labour groups on local authorities and all other definitely Labour organisations.   Most of the larger Trades Councils at the present time have a comprehensive basis, and it would certainly appear from the reports received that during the strike the most important factor in successful working was the co-ordination of all the Labour forces.   The unity then achieved could secure amazing results if it was carried into the daily work of Labour in each locality.   The best form of readiness for the future, therefore, is not the maintenance of an additional organisation (a Council of Action), but rather the transformation of the Trades Council into an all-in body, constituted and functioning on the lines of the Councils of Action during the General Strike.

In his address from the Chair at the first Trades Councils' Conference of 1925, Mr A. B. Swales, Chairman of the General Council, emphasised the need for the Trades Councils to function as the co-ordinating bodies in each locality :

" We do not want, nor would conditions permit us, to return to the narrow limitations of the Trades Councils of the past. We do not want Trades Councils to be purely strike committees and nothing else, as they were originally. We cannot afford to neglect political action, the development of our co-operatives, the movement for independent working-class education, our youths' and children's movements, our social organisations, and so on. The Trades Councils have now a wider and a more general field of operations. . . . A Trades Council to-day is really not a ' trades ' council in the old restricted craft sense, it is a council of workers' representatives from various working-class organisations—industrial, political, and in some cases co-operative—met to consider how conscious working-class action can be taken in regard to every sphere of activity."

This wide basis for the Trades Councils receives additional support when their necessary activities are examined, on the lines of the resolutions adopted at the Conference of Trades Councils.

The formation of industrial groups in the Trades Council is recommended in par. 3 (b) of the Model Rules, on the lines of the T.U.C. grouping, namely :—

Group A.—Mining and Quarrying, Railways, Transport.
,, B.—Shipbuilding, Engineering, Iron and Steel, Building.
,, C.—Cotton, Other Textiles, Clothing, Leather.
,, D.—Glass, Pottery, Distribution, etc. ; Agriculture, and General Workers.
,, E.—Printing and Paper, Public Employees, Non-Manual Workers.
,, F.—Women's Group (organisations having women members).

The grouping is not a mere formality ; it is essential for developing 100 per cent. organisation, for creating the spirit which will tend towards industrial unionism, and, in an emergency, for effective unity of action. To some extent the grouping system became operative

during the strike, through the formation of Joint Strike Committees ; but it is certainly desirable that it should become a permanent form of organisation. It is obvious that the grouping cannot be on identical lines in every Trades Council, but some form of industrial grouping, in which the groups have definite functions, is essential.

One other point of great importance in the constitution of Trades Councils is the question of the basis of representation. At the Scarborough Trades Union Congress (1925) a resolution was adopted :—

" That strong well-organised Shops Committees are indispensable weapons in the struggle to force the Capitalists to relinquish their grip on industry, and therefore pledges itself to do all in its power to develop and strengthen workshop organisation."

The resolution passed by the 1926 Conference of Trades Councils, urging the development and strengthening of organisation inside the workshops, was based on the Scarborough resolution ; but so far very little has been done in this direction, and it may be doubted whether much can be done with the machinery of the present *branch* basis of representation. Here again the strike experience serves as a pointer. The joint strike committees, formed especially for railway depots, functioned well, and were represented on the Councils of Action. The substitution of shop or depot committee representation for branch representation raises very difficult questions, but it is undoubtedly in the direction of progress, and would enormously strengthen the Trades Councils. It might be possible, as an intermediate step, to provide for representation of shop committees on the separate industrial groups of the Trades Councils. In any case, any campaign for strengthening the shop organisation should be accompanied by provision, in one form or another, for regular contact between the Trades Council and the shop committees.

THE WORK TO BE DONE.

The most essential part of the work of the Trades Councils must be systematic and unremitting efforts to secure 100 per cent. organisation—the basis for any successful defence against the employers' attacks, or for any successful move forward.   During the strike practically in every locality the Councils of Action came up against great difficulties arising from the fact that so many of the road transport workers are un-organised ; many of the reports received draw special attention to this.   But they were not the only un-organised group, and an immense field requires to be organised.   There are only some $5\frac{1}{2}$ million trade unionists, while the number of workers covered by the Insurance Acts is 11 millions, and the 1921 Census shows over 16 million workers of all grades and trades. The task of organising these workers can only partially be carried out by the trade unions themselves.   Only well-thought-out and persistent local effort, in which the workers who are well organised locally come to the assistance of the workers in the badly organised in-dustries and shops, can ensure real progress towards 100 per cent. organisation.

As for the detailed methods to be used, some are indicated in the resolution of the 1926 Conference, but obviously the nature of much of the work must depend on local circumstances.   There is one point, however, which emerges from a few of the reports, and which undoubtedly applied throughout the coun-try—the need for special efforts to secure some form of organisation for women.   In so far as women factory-workers are concerned the problems are not fundamentally different from those affecting men, although the organising of women workers, and keeping them in the organisation, is actually more difficult than in the case of men.   But women factory workers form only a small part of the total number of women in the working class, and it seems essential that, for example, efforts should be made to create organisations for the wives of trade union members.   It is true that through the women's sections of Labour Parties and through the political organisations generally, as well as the Women's Co-operative Guilds, etc., some of the more active elements are linked up with the movement. But during the strike, and in the coalfields throughout the lockout, much wider numbers came into active contact with the local movement, and the Trades Councils should aim at permanent contacts which would be of immense service in both the industrial and political fields.

In Chapter V. the question of linking up with the Co-operative movement was discussed, and this also arises out of the resolution passed by the 1925 Trades Councils Conference.   This matter needs most serious attention, as is brought out in many of the reports ; above all, it must not be regarded as something lying outside the industrial needs of the workers.   It is, in a very literal sense, a bread and butter question, and work to bring about both personal identity— every Trade Unionist a Co-operator—and organisational connection — representation on the Councils— must be one of the main activities of the Trades Councils.

The linking up of political with the industrial activities in each area is also an essential part of the work to be done.   Trade Union propaganda will have a considerable and lasting effect only if it is supplemented with propaganda aiming at the development of a consciousness of the class struggle, on which alone a live industrial movement can be based. And on the other hand the political movement in the localities must be brought in to help the industrial movement. The personal canvass for Trade Union membership suggested by the 1926 Trades Councils Conference (resolution numbered 6 (b) above) might well be the normal accompaniment of every electoral canvass. The linking up of Labour groups on local authorities with the Trades Council is vital to any real action, and the work done by Labour Borough Councils and Boards of Guardians, both during the General Strike and during the mining lock-out, shows the important part that can be played during emergencies. It should be the aim of the Trades Councils to bring Labour groups into the regular service of the local movement.

In the development of all its activities the Trades Council will find the local Labour Bulletin or paper a most valuable asset. This point, and many others, have been dealt with in the course of the preceding chapters. The building up of workers' clubs, sports' organisations, etc. ; special efforts to organise young workers ; the formation of a defence corps ; building up the nucleus of a transport organisation—all these are matters which will have to be dealt with in the task of creating an active and united local movement which will be ready for the next crisis.

It is a large programme, but the experiences of the Nine Days have shown that, under the stimulus of a crisis, the organised movement in the localities is capable of united and successful action along these lines. While, therefore, the activities which are recorded and examined in this book are those of an emergency, and while plans must be made to make such emergency activities more effective, the main lessons to be drawn from the reports are applicable to the everyday life of the Trades Councils.   The building up of Trades Council organisation and activity is the most essential part of the preparations for the struggles which lie ahead.

Success, even success in industrial organisation, can only be achieved by making the Labour movement loom so big in the lives of the workers in the locality that it meets all their needs and aspirations, and commands attention because it cannot be ignored.

REPORTS FROM TRADES COUNCILS

In Reply to Questionnaire sent
out by the Labour Research
Department after the Strike.

INDEX TO REPORTS.

TEXT OF REPORTS.

Aberdeen.

Organisation.—Central Strike Committee.

Arrangements with Co-op.—The Co-op. advanced money until cheques came along.

Special points.—The weak point with us was our system of couriers keeping us in touch with the various districts. Our organisation in Aberdeen was fairly well handled. We had our various Committees sitting. For instance, our Permit Committee received applications between the hours of 10 a.m. to 12 noon and issued permits from 2 p.m. to 5 p.m. The Central Strike Committee met every evening at 9 o'clock and often sat till 2 a.m.

Publicity.—A local sheet was issued from 6th to 12th May, as a Strike Bulletin, 5000 copies daily. It is now the *Aberdeen Citizen*, an evening paper. Up to a few days ago we were getting the paper printed by a private firm, but we have now obtained machinery of our own—one of the latest linotypes, and we are now producing our paper in our own premises.

Arrests and Defence.—No arrests were made ; no workers' defence organised.

Position on May 12.—Tram men had come out to a man. Students filled a number of places. Result, Tram men were wavering by 12th, and a number would have been back by end of week. Rail men and Dockers were good right up to end.

Accrington.

Organisation.—A full representative meeting was first of all called, which decided that all Branch Secretaries of Trade Union Organisations be called for the purpose of selecting a " Council of Action." This acted throughout the dispute.

Arrangements with Co-op.—None, except for those branches who banked with C.W.S. to have strike funds in readiness.

Special points.—Our weakness was in not being able to control successfully those transport men working for firms who only employed one or two men. The threat of dismissal in these cases often resulted in the men staying in. A few of the local newspaper men went back before the dispute ended.

Publicity.—We ran a small Bulletin. One issue each day. This is not being continued.

Arrests.—One small boy was arrested for throwing orange peel at a charabanc.

Aldershot.

Organisation.—The "Aldershot Disputes Advisory Council " was set up by the Trades Council, whose officers arranged the provisional inaugural meeting, consisting of the Secretaries and Chairmen (or other elected delegates) of Unions involved. The N.U.R., R.C.A., T. & G.W., Typographical Association, and Printing and Paper Workers, were the only Unions affected here, about 400 out here all told ; 14 still out, mostly printing and paper workers. This Advisory Council has been constituted a permanent Council at meeting held at Labour Hall, Sunday, May 16th, 1926.

Arrangements with Co-op.—Arranged for T.U. Drivers and gave Council Permits for Supplies and arranged for supplies to needy cases should it be required. Co-op. Transport men joined up. No difficulty with supplies.

Special points.—Strikers' behaviour exemplary ; great asset, our own Labour Hall—small, but very useful. The N.U.R., R.C.A., T.A., and P.P.W. were splendid and surpassed our most sanguine anticipations. Transport was quite O.K. as far as our news was concerned. The Aldershot and District Traction Coy. (Bus Coy.) ran their buses as usual, that is, except those that were commandeered. These men are totally unorganised and therefore could not do anything with them—that's our next job, to get them in. We had several strangers call at our hall and offered services of cars for transport purposes (ladies included). We were able to avail ourselves of their help on five or six occasions for running reports to Eccleston Square from surrounding districts, also to keep the spirits of strikers up as far as

Alton. Delegates were also taken by these means to Unity House, Paper Workers' Headquarters at Clapham, and R.C.A. Headquarters. One curious aspect was when three large lorries drew up at Labour Hall for Trades Council Permits. They had been to London for meat with the Food Officer's Permit, but being non-union drivers, were sent back to Aldershot *empty*. The Town Clerk (Food Officer) came post haste to Labour Hall for the Strike Committee to countersign his permits, but we would not do it without seeing the drivers, making sure that they were T.U. men and that it was food only. Later the arrangement was cancelled by us.

Publicity.—No local news-sheet issued. Labour Hall windows used for announcing important news in crayon. We obtained *British Worker* by sending up motor cyclists. 20 quires daily—40 when possible.

Workers' defence.—Was being organised when strike called off. No arrests. We set up a Distress Fund and are still looking after those who have been victimised as best we can.

Position on May 12.—No sign of weakening whatever ; stronger if anything ; few drifted back, but more came out. The mood of the men and women here who were on strike was splendid, and it was a big shock when we heard the strike was off. But we expect it was for the best, although we cannot understand it yet, as we all thought we had won.

Ashton, Stalybridge, etc.

Organisation.—Strike Committee formed of representatives of all Unions with members involved. Trades Council represented on Committee by six delegates.

Arrangements with Co-op.—Co-operative Society volunteered to honour vouchers if issued.

Special points.—Road transport workers badly organised, with result that some who came out returned before strike terminated.

Publicity.—No daily bulletin. Statement issued to Unions concerned from time to time.

Arrests, etc.—No arrests locally ; no workers' defence arrangements.

Position on May 12.—No sign of weakening apart from road transport workers, as indicated above.

Aylesbury.

Organisation.—Trades Council met but decided to leave formation of Strike Committee to the several T.U.'s involved. This was done. No permanent arrangements made.

Arrangements with Co-op.—Local Co-op. advanced the cash for first strike pay, and gave Strike Committee and all T.U.'s free use of all rooms during crisis. Fund raised to help any case of distress.

Publicity.—No local bulletin issued. Arranged for copies of the *British Worker* to be fetched from London daily.

Arrests.—None. Everything and everybody peaceful.

Bath.

Organisation.—Trades Council Executive, with one representative from each of the 19 unions in dispute acted as Bath Council of Action. A permanent Council of Action is now in force, made up as above.

Arrangements with Co-op.—None whatever.

Special points.—Co-ordination of Council of Action with Unions' Local Committees in advisory consultations. Motor cycle despatch riders with all towns 30 miles round.

Publicity.—Spasmodic bulletin at first, then daily ; 50 duplicated ; typewriter utilised with Gestetner Rotary Copier. Not to be continued.

Arrests.—None whatever ; have been complimented and thanked by Mayor and Chief Constable for maintaining perfect order ; advised Mayor first day of strike to disband local specials as superfluosities.

Bermondsey.

Organisation.—The Trades Council appointed a Council of Action, with a representative from the Strike Committees. A Sub-Committee has been formed in connection with the Miners' Relief Fund.

Arrangements with Co-op.—None.

Special points.—The Borough Council, being Labour, formed an Emergency Sub-Committee, which was in close touch with the Council of Action, and both the Town Halls were passed over to the Trades Council during the strike, which were used for Strike meetings and Strike Committees.

Publicity.—A bulletin was started the first day of the Strike and continued throughout. About 6000 copies daily. Not to be continued.

Arrests.—None. Everything very quiet in Bermondsey, one or two disturbances just on the borders of Borough and Southwark.

Position on May 12.—No signs of weakening whatever. The workers were more solid on the 12th than at the first. The spirit of the workers, both men and women, could not be better. They were just splendid. We had wonderful meetings at both Town Halls every night ; afternoon meetings for the women.

Bethnal Green.

Organisation.—Trades Council Executive took over full power. Internal re-organisation of Trades Council now taking place.

Publicity.—Local bulletin issued from second day of Strike.

Arrests.—Five arrests of Movement members and about 20-30 ordinary arrests of general crowd.

Position on May 12.—Not weakening at all. Our nightmare was always pushing second line of defence back to work.

Biggleswade and District.

Organisation.—As a Strike Committee, composed of R.C.A., N.U.R., and Nat. Union of Vehicle Builders ; all T.C. Officers on Committee.

Arrangements with Co-op.—Only hire of Hall for time of General Strike.

Special points.—Good communications and solidarity of men.

Position on May 12.—No weakening whatever.

Birkenhead.

Organisation.—E.C. of Trades Council acted as Council of Action with right of co-option.

Arrangements with Co-op.—Provision of Meeting-Rooms.

Special Points.—Worked along usual strike lines. Each Union did own picketing.

Publicity.—Local bulletin issued in conjunction with Liverpool.

Arrests.—Two.

Position on May 12.—No weakening. Stoppage was extending.

Bolton.

Organisation.—Wired to all E.C. members of Local Trades Council as Emergency Committee. Decided to form a Central Strike Committee under the title of the " Bolton Council of Action." Committee composed of the Secretary of every local Union affected directly or indirectly by the General Strike. Other secretaries were brought in as soon as they were affected. President of Trades Council appointed Chairman, and Secretary of Trades Council appointed Joint Secretary along with self. I am Labour Agent in Bolton, and, as a full-time Agent with an Office, Telephone, and Gestetner Rotary machine, was also appointed Joint Secretary. We formed the following Sub-Committees—Office Staff, Organisation, Transport, Publicity, Finance, Public Committees, Picketing, Vital Services, Messengers. All Railway Unions had, in addition, a Strike Committee, and a representative was on the above Council. All their efforts were co-ordinated by us, and the Council was the sole authoritative body all through, taking our instructions from the North Western Area Council, who in turn received theirs from the T.U.C. General Council. The Council of Action is retained in the meantime to assist in the direction of helping the Miners by a Relief Fund and the feeding of Miners' kiddies ; and helping, where possible, to secure the return to work of victimised strikers. Future of Council yet to be finally determined.

Arrangements with Co-op.—No arrangements whatever were made with the Co-operative Society. It is largely a Conservative body, and non-sympathetic. They did not offer to help us in any way at all.

Special points.—Local organisation points were many. Here are a few essentials. Powerful wireless set installed the first day of the strike. 2280 pickets mobilised in two days. Every picket did four hours on and twenty hours off. All were badged with a white silk ribbon. 29 push bikes and 57 motor bikes mobilised for picket and messenger work. Two local Cinemas granted free use of Cinemas for morning and afternoon meetings of strikers. Contact originated and maintained with practically every town in Lancashire each day. From Lancaster to Todmorden and from Macclesfield to Liverpool. No open-air meetings held at all. We kept our people off the streets as far as possible. Result—not a single *Trade Unionist* arrested in Bolton. The Chief Constable reports that crime in Bolton last week was less than any week for a number of years.

Publicity.—We ran a bulletin every day, commencing on Saturday, May 8, 1926, when we published morning, noon and evening. Published from Saturday, May 8, 1926, to Saturday, May 15, 1926, inclusive. 4000 to 5000 copies daily, a total of 38,000 copies—*free*. Not likely to be continued, as the Bolton Labour Party run a *Bolton Labour News* in similar form, which will serve local purposes.

Arrests.—In Bolton proper, none. In Little Lever, close by, in the Bolton County Area, ten lads from 17 to 22 years of age, arrested for withdrawing the draw pin of a coal cart and spilling the coal in the roadway. The man in charge of the coal cart dared them to do their worst. County Bench inflicted savage sentences up to three months. All details sent to Parliamentary Labour Party. Local Fund for taking the matter to higher court if possible. At

Farnworth, close by, one man sent to gaol for a month for tearing down a Government poster.

Bo'ness.

Organisation.—Conference called by Trades Council, and local Strike Committee appointed with full powers from all unions and for all purposes.

Arrangements with Co-op.—None of a general nature. The Co-op. Committee is composed mostly of Socialists and gave £150 to local distress.

Special Points.—Scottish T.U.C. sent all letters back to railmen's secretary instead of T.C. secretary ; all other organisation was perfect.

Arrests.—No arrests.   No disturbance of any kind.

Position on May 12.—No weakening.   All workers solid except five railwaymen, and workers not out wished to come out.

Bootle.

Organisation.—As Council of Action (Sub-Council for Bootle) under orders of Merseyside Council of Action, on which we had two delegates.

Special Points.—All essential work was done from Liverpool.

Publicity.—Merseyside bulletin issued from Liverpool.

Arrests.—None.

Position on May 12.—Some weakening among Engineers and Railway Clerks, lot went back.   N.U.G. and M.W. members never out in many cases.

Bradford and District.

Organisation.—Emergency Committee representatives from each Union, who appointed Central Executive Committee.   Will be maintained if need arises.

Arrangements with Co-op.—None.

Special points.—The organisation was excellent.   Every Union represented on Committee.

Publicity.—Local bulletin issued.   Started on Saturday, 8th May, 1926.   Three issues—10,000, 6,000, and 10,000. Not to be continued.

Arrests.—None.   Two only summoned.

Brighton and District.

Organisation. — Brighton "Council of Industries" (Trades Council) called meeting of delegates from working-class organisations.   As result, a Council of Action was formed—4 from General Council of the C. of I., 4 from Railway and Transport Strike Committee, 4 from Building Trade Strike Committee, 4 from Printing Trade Strike Committee, 4 from Labour Party, 4 from Co-op., 2 from I.L.P., 1 from Working Women's Council.   This met daily. Council of Action still in being in skeleton form, also Railway and Transport S.C. and Printing Trade S.C.

Arrangements with Co-op.—(See above).   Also granted £100 in food vouchers to local Relief Fund, also £50 in vouchers for outlying districts.

Special points.—C. of A. well attended.   R.C.A. men did good secretarial work.   Duplicators lent by Labour Party and I.L.P. duplicated T.U.C. Bulletins, and motor car and motor cyclist distributed same in outlying districts.   *Weakness*—lack of initiative for new developments. Stood strictly to T.U.C. Bulletins and instructions.   Members of C. of A. mostly of "moderate" type.   I think local C. of A. did not organise the workers on strike well enough.   Hence tendency to hang about waiting for news or rumours.   Some sports were arranged, but not by C. of A.

Publicity.—Local bulletin, *Stand Firm*, issued twice daily.   3000 copies first day ; 2000 second day.   Not to be continued.   Communist Party (Local) issued three or four editions of typewritten *The Punch*.   About 5000 copies altogether.

Defence Corps and Arrests.—Was moved in C. of A. that a "Corps of Stewards" be formed to keep order. This passed on to Strike Committees on Tuesday, May 11th ; about 300 mounted and foot police in cars came down to

Tram Depot, charged the crowd, hitting them with sticks, two feet long with knobs on the end.   Object—to get the trams out (none were running) ;   22 arrests were made. Tried next day, sentences from 1 to 6 months.   Moved in C. of A. after raid and arrests that a Workers' Defence Corps be formed of at least 500 men to protect workers' meetings, etc. ;   this was lost.   Reformists said it would make more trouble.   I.L.P. and Co-op. delegates said said they would leave C. of A. if carried.

Position on May 12.—The position can be said to have been solid, and every sign of wishing to continue struggle by the workers.   Some—a few—reported to have gone back to work.   Apparent surprise at strike being called off.

Cambridge.

Organisation.—As a Joint Emergency Committee, composed of delegates from T.C. and proportionate representation from each Union actually on strike.   Meetings morning and evening.   This Emergency Committee is not being continued, but easily re-organised if necessary.

Arrangements with Co-op.—Loan, and donation for Distress Fund.

Special points.—Slight overlapping as to speakers for places outside Cambridge at commencement, but overcome by establishing a Sub-Committee to deal with.

Publicity.—Strike bulletin started on May 6th.   Then continuously until May 13th.   Average 650 copies. Bulletin not to be continued.

Special Note from a member of Strike Committee.—A Joint Emergency Strike Committee of 30-40 persons was formed from the Trades Council, together with representatives from the Labour Party.   This met for the first time on the morning of Tuesday, the 4th, and on subsequent mornings.   It set up an Entertainments Committee, which organised concerts, lectures, church parades and tours round the University ;   and also a Publicity Committee.   The latter secured the personal assistance of members of the University Labour Club and the loan of cars, and on Thursday, the 6th, commenced arrangements for the issue of a daily Strike Bulletin. Subsequently it also organised the distribution of 15,000-20,000 copies of *The British Worker* for East Anglia (excluding Norwich). Arrangements for printing the local bulletin could not be made, and it was accordingly issued as a duplicated type-written sheet in 500-1000 copies, and was distributed in Cambridge and the surrounding villages. The editors of it were instructed to avoid mention of Government pro-vocation and of the word " Council of Action." Meetings were organised in Cambridge and surrounding towns and villages. Everywhere, even in outlying villages, the workers were solid and the spirit magnificent. Much feeling has been subsequently caused by the action of the Railway Companies, and by the refusal of the paper mills at the village of Sawston to re-employ any men who remain members of the Union.

Canterbury.

Organisation.—As the Trades Council Emergency Strike Committee. This has been kept in existence and working in co-operation with the Miners' lock-out.

Arrangements with Co-op.—To supply food, etc., to members on strike.

Special Points.—The organisation here was perfect.

Position on May 12.—No weakening whatever ; our difficulty was to keep the men not involved at work.

Castle Cary and District.

Organisation.—Our Council consists of only two Branches—N.U.R. and Workers' Union. The latter is a very small Branch, consisting exclusively of roadmen and farm labourers, none of which came out on strike, so that the local branch of the N.U.R. (about 80 members) func-tioned as Strike Committee, and while members of the T.C., apart from N.U.R. members, were frequently at their daily meetings, the T.C. did not officially function, but held itself ready to act in case of need.

Position on May 12.—No sign of weakening. The local branch of the N.U.R. still runs as previously. The N.U.R.

were solid right to the end, except for one signalman and one packer.

Castleford and District.

Organisation.—A Council of Action, including T.C. and Strike Committees affected.   No permanent organisation, but I have instructions to convene special meeting of Council when required.

Arrangements with Co-op.—Headquarters were at the Co-op. ; they lent us the rooms.

Special points.—Entertainments Committee was formed to keep the minds of the men occupied.

Publicity.—No local news-sheet issued.   I issued several circulars in thousands and got them distributed.   We also duplicated the General Council bulletins when I received them.

Arrests.—One woman and one man—both Communists. One of our local secretaries—a railwayman.   We successfully fought the case with Counsel, and he was bound over in £100 and two sureties of £100 for three months.

Chatham and District.

Organisation.—As Trades Council, co-operating with Strike Committee of representatives from branches having members out.   No permanent arrangements made.

Arrangements with Co-op.—Negotiations had taken place with the three Co-op's. in district for credits in goods for men out ; although not used, it is known that credits would have been forthcoming.

Special points.—It may be advisable to so arrange our organisation that clerical work is done by the branches catering for clerical workers.

Publicity.—No local bulletin issued.   MSS. were prepared but not used owing to the calling off.

Workers' defence.—All meetings outdoors were policed by chosen members quite successfully.   No arrests took place.

Position on May 12.—There was weakening only in one case, as a result of different interpretation of instructions by two unions.

Cheltenham.

Organisation.—All-in Council of Action.

Arrangements with Co-op.—They gave relief vouchers to distress cases.

Publicity.—No local strike sheet published; daily bulletins outside the council room, containing chief news of council and news items.

Position on May 12.—No weakening.

Cleckheaton.

Organisation.—Central Disputes Committee, consisting of Chairman and Secretary of local Trade Unions and T. & L. Council Executive. This is being maintained in existence.

Arrangements with Co-op. — None. They have since agreed that if necessity arises for miners' cases, the matter will be dealt with.

Special points.—Everything good, with the exception of transport, largely due to the number of non-unionists.

Publicity.—No local news-sheet issued, but bulletins were posted in prominent places all over the district and were very useful as news items, in addition to making the boycott of blackleg papers effective. Not to be continued.

Arrests.—None.

Clitheroe.

Organisation.—As Council of Action.

Special Points.—The special picketing of the goods-yard.

Publicity.—Took 100 sheets of the Blackburn Strike Committee.

Position on May 12.—No weakening.

Colchester.

Organisation.—Special Conference called of Trades Council, E.C. of Labour Party and General Committee. Special Strike Committee formed of two from each Union and two from Labour Party. Also special Transport

Committee of Transport Unions from above. This Committee is still in being.

Arrangements with Co-op.—Advances were being arranged when strike called off. Distress Fund Food Tickets issued through Co-op. Relationships strained over permits, as they were, after first issue, refused.

Special points.—Local organisation worked very well. Had a car full time to send out speakers and pickets to outlying places. Also many motor cycle runners.

Publicity.—Printers out here, and would not allow us to print local Labour Paper, though printed by small master-man (T.A.). About 2000 of duplicated bulletin issued on 8th, 10th, and 12th, and given free to those out. Sold at 1d to men remaining in.

Arrests and Defence.—No arrests. All steady here. No specials. Own pickets for meetings. Only police sent as asked for by us.

Coventry.

Organisation.—Anticipating a crisis in the Engineering industry, which is the principal industry in Coventry, a specially-convened meeting on 22nd April, 1926, of organisations concerned, agreed that the Trades Council E.C., together with specially co-opted persons from the different unions, should be the Council of Action in any crisis that might arise. Hence, at the call of the General Council, the Trades Council E.C. immediately functioned, and co-opted some 30 representatives from different trade unions—not necessarily involved directly. A Council of Action of about 50 was thus rapidly formed ; it did not become unwieldy, and proved a very live body. It is hoped that the Council of Action will continue to function as a trade union organising committee.

Arrangements with Co-op.—No definite arrangements were made with the Co-op., but it did play a prominent part in the struggle. It placed a car at the disposal of the Council of Action, and also gave facilities in the way of duplicating " Speakers' Notes," supplied copies of verbatim wireless reports, and generally intimated that it would do all possible to meet any demands of the Council of Action. On the other hand, the Co-op. used the Council of Action in securing permits for release of food supplies, and also in securing for them permission from the Warwickshire Miners' Association to obtain a supply of coal for domestic purposes from one of the local pits. The Co-op. also played an important part in controlling prices. At a meeting of tradesmen and Trades Council representatives on Monday, 3rd May, convened by the local Food Controller, the chairman of the Co-op. intimated that for at least 14 days there would be no increase. The local vultures were obviously bitterly disappointed. The same is true of the coal previously mentioned. The permission secured from the Warwickshire Miners' Association made it possible for a share of the coal which would otherwise have been handled by private merchants (transport and distributive trade generally being badly organised outside the Co-op. and trams) to be given to the Co-op., which stated that the price would be 2/3 ; and again the merchants, who had visions of 3/- and 3/6, were defeated—2/3 became the general price. The important part of the Co-operative Societies cannot be too much emphasised, and everything possible should be done to fix up arrangements for the next round.

Special points.—Only a review of the work attempted can satisfactorily answer this question. In the first place the response to the call was magnificent ; throughout the whole of the dispute only one section was weak, and this section was not involved until nearly the end. The political organisation ceased to function as such, and placed their resources at the disposal of the Council of Action. A Publications and Publicity Committee was appointed for the issuing of bulletins, distribution of *British Workers*, and general propaganda. This Committee had the services of competent voluntary sign writers. A Transport Committee controlled all transport for despatch riding, etc. A timed service was gradually being worked out which would have linked up the whole of the district. Nine cars and about 60 motor cycles (solos and combinations) were offered to us, petrol costs only being asked. Arrangements were also being made to have qualified engineers available to attend to T.U.C. cars or motor cycles if necessary.   A Distress Committee was appointed.   All collections at meetings were given for this purpose.   The committee is now giving special attention to raising funds for the miners of the Warwickshire coalfield.   A Meetings' Committee did good work, not only in Coventry, but in the wider area in its charge.   A Socials' Committee, with a Musicians' Union organiser as secretary, did good work. A Permits' Committee controlled the work of Trade Unionists involved in the movement of supplies, and also reviewed all other cases where doubt was expressed as to the requirements of the General Council.   Any weaknesses were due to the inherent weakness of the general standing of Trades Councils throughout the country, and to the lack of sufficiently frequent and clear instructions from the General Council.   Also, the prime weakness lay in the fact that instructions to cease work and to re-start came from National Executives and not the General Council.   The strength of the organisation lay in the ready help that was forthcoming and in the surprising capacity of the workers to organise.   Trades Councils have never met with the support they ought to have had, and consequently Trades Council organisation, which was the organisation which the General Council in the main relied upon for its propaganda and general unifying of the strike, is, to say the least, somewhat scrappy.   Coventry is no exception, and the tasks and problems set the Coventry Council of Action were exceedingly varied, and, it is believed, important.   Centres like Rugby and Crewe would, in the main, be confined to the rail side of the dispute. Big cities like Manchester and Birmingham would have complicated issues, but have relatively good organisation. With its scanty organisation and previous equipment, Coventry was linked up with every phase of the dispute (excepting dockers)—railways, transport (trams), engineering, printing, distribution (N.U.D.A.W.), power, and building trades.   In addition, Coventry was made a centre by the General Council for the distribution of propaganda, etc., to Rugby, Warwick, Leamington, Nuneaton, Hinckley, and Bedworth. Also, at the outset of the dispute, Coventry took over from Nuneaton some half-dozen colliery and railway villages, and also found it necessary to cover a number of *ther villages which had not been specifically allotted to it. The vague definitions of the first memorandum relating to engineering and transport set Coventry a difficult problem at the outset, viz., to what extent is the manufacture of motor cars transport ? Coventry settled it by calling her engineers out *before* the general call to engineers. Other difficulties were, to what extent assistance should be given to the local Food Controller, extent of permits for the movement of food supplies, the E.T.U. cinema operators wanted to know if they would be in order in using " black " juice—many of the difficulties could have been easily dealt with if the Council of Action had been supplied with a statement which would have laid down general principles, and to which reference could have been made.

Publicity.—The Publicity Committee issued a number of Strike Bulletins, but here there certainly appears to have been a weakness, inasmuch as adequate copies do not appear to have been filed. Where a supply of *British Workers* was expected in the morning, a bulletin would be issued in the evening and vice versa. About 200 of each issue were duplicated. It will not be continued, because a *Labour Monthly* was already being published before the strike.

Crewe.

Organisation.—Functioned as a General Strike Committee, composed of delegates from every Trade Union Branch and the officials of the Trades Council. The Central Strike Committee is still in existence, but only until our Distress Fund is worked out. Afterwards the Industrial Committee of the Trades Council will be put into proper form.

Arrangements with Co-op.—Credit was arranged for members up to half their share capital.

Publicity.—A bulletin sheet was issued daily from the first day until the end of the General Strike. About 200 copies daily. It is not being continued.

Arrests.—None. There have been a few cases of intimidation, but as a whole we were on good terms with the police.

Position on May 12.—No sign of weakening whatever.

Croydon.

Organisation.—The Trade Union Council of the Croydon Labour Party constituted itself a Council of Action for the period of the strike, with power to co-operate with other bodies. A Central Strike Committee was set up consisting of representatives of the Council of Action and of all T.U. branches on strike. For the future, this Strike Committee can be set up under T.U.C. whenever necessary.

Arrangements with Co-op.—See under " Special Points."

Special points.—Absolute solidarity. Closest co-operation between political and industrial wings of the Party. (The local T.U.C. is a Committee of the Croydon Labour Party and all T.U. delegates to the Party's General Council. Practically every T.U. branch affected is affiliated). No friction between right and left wings. Running of Strike Bulletin, printed by voluntary T.U. labour, under direction of local Printing Trades Strike Committee. Running of monster demonstration—the largest Croydon has ever seen. Running of many concerts and other social events free to strikers, under direction of Mr. Rutland Boughton and Socials' Committee. Running of Propaganda Meetings (indoor and outdoor). Both prospective Parliamentary Candidates were very prominent. Organisation of Workers' Defence Corps to keep order, etc. (will be made permanent). Centralisation of organisation in suitable premises (Ruskin House). Organisation of dispatch department, with adequate volunteers (cyclists, motor cyclists and motor cars). Opening of buffet for strikers at Ruskin House under direction of Labour Party's Social Committee. Opening of Distress Fund. Sale of *British Worker*, which we fetched each day from London. There were no bad points locally—except that the workers haven't captured the Co-op. yet (a campaign to effect this was opened previous to strike and is proceeding).

Publicity.—Local Strike Bulletin published (see " Special Points ") from May 8th, for 4 days.   2000 to 3000 copies. Not to be continued ; the Croydon Labour Party normally runs a monthly publication.

Defence.—See " Special Points."

Darlington.

Organisation.—Council of Action brought into being by the Local Trades Council.   It ceased to function immediately the T.U.C. called off the strike.

Arrangements with Co-op.—None.

Special points.—None worth mentioning, except that we were responsible for extra good order.   Our Borough Member, Mr. A. Shepherd, M.P., co-operated splendidly with all matters during the strike ; in fact, the demonstration on the Sunday, 8th May, was two miles long ; he did yeoman service and I am wishful to record same.

Publicity.—The local N.U.R. people ran a local Strike Bulletin ; this varied, as they were duplicated.   Not to be continued ; we have a permanent local Labour Monthly.

Arrests.—None.

Dartford.

Organisation.—As Council of Action, composed of delegate from each Trade Union having members in the area.   We found this course best, because we had Trade Union membership but without branches in the area.   It is decided to maintain the organisation.

Arrangements with Co-op.—None direct.   See *re* Dartford Divisional Trades Council, to which we were affiliated.

Special points.—The General Workers and Municipal Workers' Union and the Public Works and Constructional Operatives' Union were entirely without instructions from their Executives.

Publicity.—No local sheet issued.   We were directed in local matters by the minutes of the Divisional Trades Council and on the wider issue by the *British Worker*.

Arrests.—None.

Note.—These remarks are confined to Stone and Swanscombe T.C. area.   The T.C. became a Council of Action, but still affiliated to the Dartford Divisional Trades Council, which was formed some time back, and representing by affiliation the Erith, Dartford, Bexley, Crayford, Stone and Swanscombe and Orpington Trades Councils.   Through this organisation we were able to maintain uniformity of action and propaganda in the whole of the Dartford Parliamentary constituency.   I believe, or I am convinced, that an organisation would be most effective in every Parliamentary division.   This would relieve the central body of a tremendous amount of work.   The central body would maintain contact with the Divisional body, and the Divisional body contact with the area Council of Action or the local Trades Council.   When I, as Secretary of the local Trades Council, received the reports from the Trade Union Congress Executive Council, we had no means to duplicate the message in leaflet form and distribute.   Alternatively, we had two halls at our disposal, and were able to hold two meetings in the noon part of the day.   At those meetings a member of the Council of Action would read the reports and any other information by minute of the Divisional Trades Council to the strikers and sympathisers assembled.   We realised from the strikers directly that the information imparted in that direct form, without any suspicion of being added to or otherwise, was most highly appreciated.   Then our meetings were continued by addresses from local speakers.

Special Note from Dartford Divisional Labour Party.

Conduct of Dispute.—The conduct of the dispute was in the hands of the Dartford Divisional Trades Council, which was a body composed of delegates elected from the local Trades Councils (5 in number), augmented by branch secretaries whose organisations were not affiliated bodies but whose members were on strike. The area of the Divisional body was co-terminous with the Dartford Parliamentary Division. It was recognised by the T.U.C. and its main functions were to co-ordinate the activities of all Trades Councils and to secure uniform administration of the T.U.C. policy as well as to interpret that policy and to give decisions on matters arising therefrom. Their main sub-committees dealt with Transport, Relief, Literature and Propaganda, Picketing, Prices ; and in the first place each sub-committee dealt with its own affairs and made recommendations thereon to the central body. The local Trades Councils worked from this central body and were subject to its instructions. Each Trades Council was responsible for its own area and had a number of small sub-committees almost identical with the sub-committees of the Divisional body. A Strike Bulletin was issued a few days before the close of the dispute. It was produced from a duplicator and sold at 1d. It was produced by the Erith Trades Council.

Communication.—We had an army of scouts, messengers, who were equipped with bicycles, motor bicycles and cars, and who were organised to work from different stations. By the fourth day of the dispute we were linked up with London and all adjacent districts. As the strike proceeded this work became more efficient.

Impressions.—Had the strike lasted another fortnight, we should have had a rent strike here. In the conduct of a General Strike, I am of the opinion it is necessary to have a Divisional Trades Council formed as an intermediate link between the Local and National organisations so as to secure uniform interpretation and administration of policy over as wide an area as possible. Industrial unionism is a necessary corollary to the General Strike weapon, so that men in each industry should be subject to the same domestic policy and receive the same strike pay. It would be even better if all strikers received the same strike pay. Differentiation in domestic policy and strike pay militated against the smooth working of the dispute and led to differences between the men. The men were not actuated by any revolutionary feelings. They felt they were fighting the Government to get a fair deal for the miners upon the basis of no reduction in wages and no increase in hours. On that issue the men were solid and their enthusiasm was white-heat. But on the revolutionary issue they were cold. (The English are not imaginative enough to produce revolutions). After the third day of the strike, if you spoke about the coalowners the audience would listen with a polite indifference, but if you attacked the Government, or even mentioned the word, you had the audience with you and that with cheers and wild enthusiasm. The issue was the T.U.C. and the Government ; the miners and the owners were secondary to this issue. I am convinced that the General Strike is a fine political weapon for Labour, provided we have a good case and faced with a reactionary Government. The instructions of the T.U.C. were accepted without question and the faith and confidence of the men in that body was a religion. I should have said the men came out solidly here and they remained so until the end. It was a great beginning, but a pitiable ending. The men returned to work humiliated, and they felt they had been deceived. I should have said that the strike has strengthened the Labour Party in this Division, and I have no doubt that if the Division was fought to-day, we should have no difficulty in returning a Labour Candidate.

Darwen.

Organisation.—As a Council of Action, including Strike Committees. This is being maintained ; we have decided to meet at intervals.

Special Points.—Means of communication had at outset developed ; later Local Courier service developed.

Publicity.—Local Sheet issued from May 9th, three days. 250, increased to 500 each day.

Position on May 12.—Weakening in one section only who were weak to begin with ; otherwise sound.

Deeside.

Organisation.—As Joint Committee of all Trade Unions. Not to be continued.

Arrangements with Co-op.—None.

Special points.—Organisation was splendid.

Publicity.—No local bulletin, but were supplied with daily bulletin, issued by Chester Trades Council.

Position on May 12.—No sign of weakening. Members were surprised at sudden collapse.

Denny and Dunipace.

Organisation.—As Trades Council at first. Later as Strike Committee. Maintained for organising benefits, football, etc., for miners.

Arrangements with Co-op.—Co-op. gives relief cases dividend on lines, in shape of food (extra).

Special Points.—Want of information at first. Were not notified where instructions were to come from.

Publicity.—Used bulletins from Falkirk.

Defence Corps.—Yes, but were invisible. No arrests.

Position on May 12.—No weakening.

Derby and District.

Organisation.—The Trades Council and the Local Labour Party's E.C. acted as a general Strike Committee, with two representatives from the following trades—*i.e.*, Printing, Building, Engineering, Railways and Transport, Railway Carriage and Wagon Shops Committee, Railway Allied Engineering Shops Committee. The above Committee was divided up in the following sub-committees, *i.e.*, Engineering, Transport, Dispatch, Distress, Publicity, Sports, and Entertainment. The committee has not yet been disbanded.

Arrangements with Co-op.—For the issuing of Food Vouchers on the guarantee of the respective Trade Unions.

Special points.—The organisation was good, except the misunderstandings regarding T.U.C. decisions with road transport.

Publicity.—Local bulletin was issued from the first day of the strike until the last. It was sold to the local newsboys at 13 copies for one shilling, and sold by them as a newspaper at one penny per copy. The income received for the 10 days was £92 17s 2d. It has not been issued in any form since the strike ended.

Arrests and Defence.—No arrests were made. No arrangements for defence. The L.M.S. have had two prosecutions against their employees, but both have failed in the local Police Court.

Position on May 12.—There were no signs of weakening. On the other hand more workers were coming out and joining the strike.

Doncaster and District.

Organisation.—The Council had a Council of Action representing all affiliated bodies and the C. of A. took charge entirely. In practice it broke down immediately because of lack of direct instructions, but it acted as co-ordinating link, until the 8th, when it resumed entire control of the situation locally and was served faithfully by the separate rail and transport sections. The C. of A. ceased to function immediately the General Strike was called off, and the E.C. of the Trades Council meets daily to meet any situation that may arise ; I myself have been put on full time and shall visit the whole of the area allotted to us by T.U.C. as soon as we have settled the question of arrested members.

Arrangements with Co-op.—The local society declined to give any credits whatever. Facilities for transport of foodstuffs were granted to them alone in this area.

Special points.—Response to the call wonderful. The people accepted as true only our bulletins. Scab press taboo. All prepared to go to any length if the T.U.C. instructed, but lack of definite instructions. All our communications were signed by definite officials.

Publicity.—Local bulletins issued.

Arrests.—A number arrested and sentenced ; we are appealing.

Dorking and District.

Organisation.—The N.U.R., being the largest unit, acted separately as a Strike Committee.

Special points.—Bad ; the ignoring of this Trades Council. No arrangements with Co-op. No local bulletins issued.

Arrests.—None.

Position on May 12.—A little weakening.

Dunfermline.

Organisation.—A Council of Action was formed prior to the strike, but somehow great objection was made against the name ; therefore we had to change the name to Strike Committee, under the direct control of our Council. No arrangements have been made to continue it in existence, but we are asked by the General Council of the Scottish Trades Union Congress to try and keep the committee in being for the purpose of putting their Trade Union Organisation Scheme in operation.

Arrangements with Co-op.—None ; we have great difficulty at times with certain members of the Board of Management, owing to their not even being Trade Unionists themselves, and they seem to oppose any joint action.

Special points.—Certain Trade Unions seem to be afraid to put their business in the hands of the Trades Council ; they stood aloof and information was very difficult to ascertain as to how they were progressing.

Publicity.—From the second day of the strike we issued a bulletin twice daily of about 100 copies and we carried on until the 15th May.

Arrests and Defence.—There have been a good number of arrests ; as for the exact number I am not in a position to state. In the Dunfermline area I think it has been the worst in Scotland. No arrangements were made for workers' defence.

Position on May 12.—Some sections were showing signs of weakness.

Durham.

Organisation.—The Divisional Labour Party did not act as a Council of Action, but in a number of places in its area local Councils of Action were formed, *e.g.*, Durham City, Bearpark, Ushaw Moor.

Special points.—Nothing out of the ordinary ; picketing and dispatch riding were features.

Publicity.—No local bulletin issued.

Arrests.—None.

East Ardsley and District.

Organisation.—As Council of Action, including Strike Committee. It is being kept intact for six months.

Arrangements with Co-op.—We had Co-op. directors on the Strike Committee and got good local facilities for food and money, etc.

Publicity.—No local sheet issued.

Arrests.—None.

Position on May 12.—No sign of weakening. Did not agree to return to work until May 16th, 1926, and only after pressure.

Eastbourne.

Organisation.—As Council of Action. Composed of one representative from each organisation concerned in the dispute, and the officers of the Trades Council were the officers of the Council of Action. The organisation has been maintained exactly as on the first day. They pledged themselves to stand by each other, and that has been their business, since the call off. A number were not reinstated. Funds are collected each week ; the Council meet every Friday and divide among those who are still out the money so collected.

Publicity.—We did not publish a sheet of our own. We had volunteers who fetched the *British Worker* from London. They left Eastbourne about 6 p.m. and arrived back between 7 and 8 p.m. Later they were distributed from Brighton. We got them from there, and supplied Hastings and Bexhill and the various villages. Some days we dealt with 100 quires.

Position on May 12. Not the slightest sign of weakening. We were, in fact, getting stronger. We held the whole of our men until the Monday in the hope of getting all back with no victimisation. N.U.R., R.C.A., and A.S.L.E. & F. also stood out, and the whole of the building trades.

Edmonton.

Organisation.—The Labour Party, in conjunction with the Industrial Section, formed an Emergency Strike Committee of the Joint Executives, on Friday, April 30th. On Thursday, May 6th, an aggregate meeting of Trade Unionists on strike was called together, and two representatives from each of the different industries affected were added, with one representative from the National Unemployed Workers' Committee Movement. This full committee, to the number of 30, met the next day and formed a Strike Sub-Committee of 9 ; subsequently another aggregate meeting was called and 24 were elected to form Publicity and Social Sub-Committees ; the other members who were mostly representing the political and industrial sections of this Party were shelved. It has been proposed to make this committee as constituted a permanent Council of Action, but up to the present the proposal has been defeated. We fail to see how such could function in normal times, as there would be no organisation to which it would be responsible.

Arrangements with Co-op.—It was impossible to make any arrangement with the London Co-operative Society, as they were more severely hit by the Transport and General Workers' Union than any other firm. Trading firms (ordinary) were assisted by the Government to the greatest possible extent. The Co-operative Societies were not, and the action of the Trade Unions in further hampering the distribution of food supplies by these societies was much resented in this district.

Special points.—As far as local organisation went it was quite satisfactory, but the organisation of the trade unions which had no local branches was bad. The worst were the Printing trades, who had only branches in London.

Edmonton is but a dormitory, and with the cessation of transport, their members could not get into touch, and though we used the 'phone extensively on their behalf we could get little information, and had to improvise signing sheets for their use.   It is hoped that, as the outcome of these difficulties, those unions will affiliate their residential membership in order that we may be in touch with them.

Publicity.—We issued three Strike Bulletins.   Issues by Tottenham and the *British Worker* covered most of our ground.   It will not be continued, but the Party may contrive to issue a monthly sheet.

Arrests.—Unfortunately there were four members of the Passenger section of the Transport and General Workers arrested for interfering with the trams when the Metropolitan Tramways Co. tried to get some into running order, and were subsequently sentenced to one month's hard labour without the option of a fine.   It was a regrettable occurrence, as the effort to run the trams proved a lamentable failure ;   four that came out did not complete the journey, and returned the worse for the adventure.   No other arrests were made in this district, good order being maintained.

Erith.

Organisation.—Our Party acted as follows :—The E.C. of the Local Party, with the Secretaries of all Trade Union branches, formed themselves into the local Strike Committee.   It is not to be maintained.   The reason is that the Local Party meets fairly frequently, every fortnight, and the E.C. of the Party meets the Thursday before Party meetings.

Arrangements with Co-op.—None.

Special points.—The only thing that we have to complain about is that we never had close enough contact with the T.U.C. General Council.

Publicity.—Local bulletin issued from May 11th, 1926, for seven days.   450 copies.   No definite arrangements to continue it, but the Local Party is getting down to ways and means of publishing a local paper.

Arrests and Defence.—Two arrests, but these were discharged at Dartford Police Court.   No workers' defence organised.

Position on May 12.—No sign of weakening; but disappointed at the way the strike terminated ; the majority of the workers never returned until May 24th, owing to the employers' attitude in not taking all the men back together.

Finsbury.

Organisation.—As Council of Action, which was composed of members of the Trades Council E.C., and of E.C. members of the Labour Party.   The same organisation is to be still kept in existence.

Arrangements with Co-op.—None ;   the local Co-op. was not very sympathetic.

Special points.—Hot refreshment for all-night pickets is desirable, and more members might offer rest-rooms for pickets between spells of duty.

Publicity.—A local bulletin issued, and got fined £15 for same.   Copies were duplicated and sent to local branch Strike Committee every four hours with latest news. Police have all our sets.   Not being continued.   We publish a monthly paper.

Defence and Arrests.—No workers' defence organised. Six arrests.

Position on May 12.—Decidedly no signs of weakening.

Gateshead.

Organisation.—Labour Council and E.C. formed Council of Action.   Represented on Area Central Strike Committee.   Local Strike Committee also formed.   Only the General Strike Committee at Newcastle is being maintained.

Arrangements with Co-op.—None.

Publicity.—Printed *British Worker* locally ;   only two editions.

Glastonbury.

Organisation.—As Strike Committee with N.U.R. and R.C.A. branches, they being the only workers affected in this district.   Not being kept in existence.

Arrangements with Co-op.—None.

Special points.—We had members who kept us in touch with outlying districts each day, being able to cover many miles with motor cycles.

Publicity.—No local bulletin issued.

Arrests.—No arrests in this district at all.

Position on May 12.—95 members of N.U.R. and R.C.A., being the only ones affected, were very solid, and would rather have continued the fight for miners' cause.

Gorton.

Organisation.—As Trades Council of Action, with representatives of Unions affected. Still remains a Council of Action.

Arrangements with Co-op.—Transport section were able to obtain 10/- worth of credit on presentation of voucher, from Droylésden Co-op.

Special points.—Transport Section formed to deal with all questions of transport.

Publicity.—No local bulletin issued.

Arrests.—One Communist sentenced to six months ; has appealed, and remains out on bail. Five members of Young Communist League arrested, but discharged for lack of evidence.

Guildford.

Organisation.—Council of Action. To be maintained.

Arrangements with Co-op.—Vouchers were issued, the Trades Council being responsible to Co-op., and the branches to the Trades Council.

Publicity.—Local sheet started on Tuesday, and was issued for three days. 400 daily.

Great Harwood.

Organisation.—Trades Council worked in conjunction with a Strike Committee. No permanent organisation.

Special points.—Only about 120 men concerned ; everything worked smoothly.

Publicity.—Made arrangements to issue bulletins on the last evening.

Position on May 12.—Four Transport workers returned on the 12th.

Gwauncaegurwen.

Organisation.—As Council of Action, including the industrial representatives of all affiliated Unions and Women's sections. This organisation will be maintained for all future purposes.

Arrangements with Co-op.—Co-op. represented on Council.

Special points.—The " call " on all occasions was well responded to.

Publicity.—Local bulletin issued from third day until General Strike declared off.

Hampshire and Isle of Wight.

In reply to your circular questionnaire of 17th inst., dealing with activities of organisation during the strike, I have to inform you that, owing to the enormous area covered by the Hampshire and Isle of Wight Labour Federation, no organised work was undertaken. All officers of the Federation were working in their appropriate locality. As Secretary, I placed my services at the disposal of the T.U.C. and was employed in maintaining communication between London and South Wales, carrying members of Parliament and speakers, visiting the various Strike Committees, and taking the stereos of the *British Worker* from Carmelite Street to Gloucester, Newport and Cardiff for the local editions printed in South Wales.

Halifax.

Organisation.—Council of Action formed by Trades Council, all trades represented, also each Society formed its Strike Committee. Council of Action will remain in existence for any future action.

Arrangements with Co-op.—None.

Special points.—Organisation worked well, very successful in demonstrating working-class solidarity.

Publicity.—We issued bulletins each day and sent them by carrier to towns up to 16 miles distant, letting them know the local position.   No continuance considered to be necessary.

Arrests.—Three.   Sentenced to one month hard labour in each case.

Hampstead.

Organisation.—The E.C. of the Labour Party (which functions as a T.C.), plus delegates from T.U. branches that were not affiliated, assumed control.   Efforts have been made to secure affiliation from T.U. branches, and E.C. of Party resumes activity.

Arrangements with Co-op.—Food was supplied by the local Co-op. to necessitous cases upon vouchers issued by our Distress Fund Committee.

Publicity.—" Hampstead Strike Bulletin," issued May 6th until May 13th.   Eight issued.   No arrangements for continuation.

Arrests.—A member arrested on Sunday, 16th May, at the White Stone Pond, Hampstead Heath, for referring to a report that troops in Hamilton, Scotland, refused to parade in mining areas with rifles.   Fined £15 (alternative being one month's imprisonment with hard labour).   Other arrests were made at Cricklewood, of which I have no particulars.

Harwich and District.

Organisation.—Functioned as Trades Council in the ordinary form.   Our Strike Joint Committee is to live for one year, but it is independent of and apart from the Trades Council.

Arrangements with Co-op.—Trades Council received very generous credit facilities from Co-op. (for Co-op. members only, owing to the fear of rationing being instituted).

Publicity.—Strike Committee sent motor cyclists to near branches, with just rough messages telling of our solidarity.   Cheery, and humorous telling of scabs in a muddle on our railway.   Now discontinued.

Arrests.—None.

Position on May 12.—Signs of weakening ; a good few had gone back to work.

Special Note.—The B.B.C. had a most demoralising effect on our womenfolk, which reacted on their men.

Hebden Bridge.

Organisation.—Local Emergency Committee.   Not to be maintained.

Arrangements with Co-op.—Permits for the distribution of foodstuffs.

Publicity.—Railway Strike Bulletin, Friday, 5th-7th May.   No copies left.   This is not being continued.

Arrests.—None.

Position on May 12.—No signs of weakening.

Hendon.

Organisation.—Trades Council only just formed, and strike run by a Joint Strike Committee, representative of all the Unions involved.   Not yet disbanded, but not likely to remain in existence as Trades Council should be functioning.

Publicity.—Bulletin run for five days—May 7 to 12th. About 600 copies each issue.   Now starting a four-page monthly.

Arrests.—Two.

Hereford.

Organisation.—As Emergency Committee and Distress and Local Transport Committees.   This will be appointed yearly.

Arrangements with Co-op.—Two of the Committee were co-opted in an advisory capacity.

Special Points.—Catering arrangements excellent ; food day and night for despatch riders and pickets.

Publicity.—Local bulletin issued, two numbers.

Ilford and District.

Organisation.—The Trades Council appointed a Joint Action Committee before the strike, which became the local Central Strike Committee on May 4th.   Not intended to maintain it permanently, but Joint Action Committee not entirely disbanded.

Arrangements with Co-op.—None practical.   Two members of local Co-op. Political Council elected to serve on Joint Action Committee as Advisory delegates.

Publicity.—No local bulletin issued.

Arrests.—Two.

Position on May 12.—No sign of weakening.

Ilkeston (Derbyshire).

Organisation.—All trades acted together as a Central Strike Committee.   Miners' lock-out still on and now controlled by Committee of Derbyshire Miners' Association.

Arrangements with Co-op.—None, but both the Society and employees are contributing handsomely to Distress Fund.

Publicity.—Local sheet issued from May 9th.   Not to be continued.

Arrests.—None.

Position on May 12.—No weakening whatever.   Stronger than ever on that date.   Spirit shown here splendid. Miners are still solid.   Police very good and sooner assisted than interfered with us.   Ilkeston is spending £1000 per week in out-relief, and 1000 children are being fed by the Education Authority.

Johnstone and District.

Organisation.—Joint Strike Committee, including Trades Council.

Arrangements with Co-op.—None ;   were negotiating with same when strike was called off.

Special points.—Local organisation was very good ; nothing extraordinary worth noting.   Never before has such solidarity been shown in an industrial dispute in this locality ;   even our political opponents, Orangemen, being active pickets and taking part generally in the struggle.

Publicity.—No local bulletin.

Arrests.—None.

Position on May 12.—Transport (Tramways), great breakaway. Majority re-started. All others 100 per cent. solid out.

Keighley.

Organisation.—Joint Strike Committee. A small Industrial Committee is always in existence to focus activities.

Arrangements with Co-op.—Tried to make arrangement, but Co-op. declined.

Special points.—Rail Clerks aloofness from Strike Committee bad. An efficient band of despatch riders to bring in and take out news of the position (good).

Publicity.—No local paper issued.

Kettering.

Organisation.—Mainly, we at Kettering acted as an ordinary Trades Council. I, as Secretary, represented our Council on all Strike Committees, so as to keep in constant touch with events, and immediately summon the Council should occasion arise. All activities of a nature that concerned all unions, or in which the help of all unions was needed, were thus transferred directly from the Strike Committees to the Trades Council without undue loss of time. The Strike Committee have dissolved on resuming work, but could be called together again should occasion arise almost immediately. The Distress Committee is the only part of the strike organisation actually in existence.

Arrangements with Co-op.—None.

Special points.—One very good point in the organisation was the arrangements for keeping the strikers together ; a large hall was taken, and although the Railway Unions (these being the largest body out) were actually responsible for this, all strikers were welcomed. General meetings were held mornings at 11 o'clock, evenings at 6.30 ; the evening meeting was followed always by a concert ; women's meeting in the afternoon ; and mass meetings on the Sunday were also good. A further hall was taken with the object of keeping together all who had to cease work as a result of the strike, each hall coming under separate committees. Arrangements were in hand to link up the committee at each hall under the Trades Council, who had this in hand.

Publicity.—No local bulletin. Only a daily report to the T.U.C. General Council.

Kilmarnock.

Organisation.—E.C. of Trades Council, together with one delegate from each trade involved, formed Central Strike Committee. This is not being maintained. We have reverted to original form of organisation.

Arrangements with Co-op.—No special arrangements.

Publicity.—No local bulletin issued.

Position on May 12.—Not the slightest sign of weakening.

King's Lynn.

Organisation.—Council of Action. This includes Spalding, Sleaford, March, Oundle, King's Lynn and Bourne, as instructed by T.U.C. Joint Strike Committee of all Unions outside transport, and central body of whole movement. Not being maintained.

Arrangements with Co-op.—No special arrangements. Working between both parties *re* permits very amicable.

Special points.—Working in connection with police authorities very good.

Publicity.—Local bulletin issued from 5th to 12th inclusive. About 60 copies each issue. Not being continued.

Arrests.—None. No trouble whatever.

Position on May 12.—All men of all grades as solid on 12th as 3rd of May.

Leeds.

Organisation.—Trades Council Executive and Council of Action acted as one committee. Officials and representatives of unions concerned acted separately as another committee, but a number of people sat on both. Committees are still in existence, but really nothing is doing, apart from raising funds to help distressed and victimised workers.

Arrangements with Co-op.—None.

Special points.—Nothing particular.   One responsible Strike Committee would have been preferable.

Publicity.—We normally produce a local weekly. During the strike a typed bulletin was issued, average about 1000 daily.   A printed bulletin was issued two days— 5000 and 12,000 respectively ;   and the *British Worker* one day (last day of strike), circulation about 7000.   Continued as before strike as our local Labour weekly—*Leeds Weekly Citizen.*

Arrests.—Cannot say definitely, but about 10 or 12— nothing serious.

Leigh.

Organisation.—As Council of Action jointly with Strike Committee.   The Council is still in being, but in reality the Trades Council is the controlling body.

Arrangements with Co-op.—The Leigh Co-op. Society, which has about 13,000 members, is allowing 20 per cent. credit in groceries, but full amount of bread and milk.

Special points.—None.   The Trades Council E.C. kept very closely in touch with the Council of Action.

Publicity.—Bulletins were issued every day without charge, and were eagerly sought after.   Started on the first day and continued until the last day when General Strike was called off.   Number varied from 100 to 300 as needed.   It was similar to the Liverpool one, and posted in prominent places.

Arrests.—One arrest for lifting bag of coal from lorry and charges (under E.P.A.) with inciting others to tip lorry over.   Fined 20/-.   No other cases.   Considering that there are thousands of miners locked out, all is very quiet.   Practically all are supporting policy of A. J. Cook, and determined to stand out.

Leyton.

Organisation.—President, two Vice-Presidents, Secretary, Asst. Secretary, Finance Committee of four members,

Postal Sorters (2 members), Transport Officer and Asst. (12 motor bikes, 2 motor cars, numerous push bikes) ; Organiser of Meetings, also of Concerts ; Captain of Pickets and Asst. ; Doorkeeper, Typist.   All communications to be signed by the President or Secretary.   Divide responsibility between the Chiefs of the Sections and don't let anyone assume supreme authority.   Executive Committee the governing body, to which all chiefs reported.   Present activity—to get non-affiliated branches to affiliate.

Arrangements with Co-op.—None.

Special points.—Find work for as many as possible ; make different people responsible for each section of your organisation.

Publicity.—A small sheet was issued, about 500 copies for eight days ; not to be continued ; distributed as soon as obtained.

Arrests.—None, very pleasant relationship with the police.

Lichfield and District.

Organisation.—Council of Action formed representative of all the Unions.   Not being maintained.

Arrangements with Co-op.—None.

Special points.—This district is small and scattered and very Conservative.   Immediately the General Strike was declared I got in touch with all the unions affected.   The special point was to keep the members interested and find them something to do.   Thanks to the N.U.R., who were by far the largest Union (68), meetings were held twice daily with special speakers.   Only about a dozen builders were affected and only six printers.   With the consent of the N.U.R., I got these to attend the meetings, and I think there was some sign of wavering until I had persuaded them to come.   Afterwards there was none whatever.   It has been the best example of solidarity Lichfield has ever seen, and I think has been the means of cementing us closer together, and goodness knows we need it.

Publicity.—No local bulletin.

Position on May 12.—No sign of weakening.   See under " Special Points."

Lincoln.

Organisation.—The Trades Council appointed a Vigilance Committee, representative of each T.U. affected, one per branch. The various sub-committees are still meeting and can be called together instantly.

Arrangements with Co-op.—The Co-op. agreed to give credit to the strikers, and were agreed on helping in·whatever direction they could.

Special points.—The answer to the call as far as Trade Unionists were concerned was 100 per cent.

Publicity.—Local bulletin issued from Thursday, May 6th, for 5 days. First day, 1000, and 2000 each subsequent edition. Not being continued. We have a local weekly Labour paper.

Arrests.—None—perfect order was kept.

Defence.—Owing to our previous Labour Representation on the City Council, we had a fairly strong influence on city affairs, and the police asked us to supply the whole of the Special Constables—which we did. The Chief has been a consistent friend of Labour and absolutely refused the assistance of either military or mounted police, which were offered and pressed on the city. In fact, they tried to impeach the Chief, but by his firmness and straight-dealing, he turned the tables on our opponents.

Littleborough.

Organisation.—As Council of Action. All Unions now represented on Trades and Labour Council.

Arrangements with Co-op.—Tentative issue of credit tickets.

Publicity.—Utilised bulletin issued by Rochdale.

Position on May 12.—No weakening.

London.

Organisation.—On April 29 the Executive of the Council decided to form itself into a Council of Action for the Greater London Area ; all District Secretaries of Unions involved to be called to a Joint Meeting, and all local Trades Councils to be called to a Special Conference to decide on common lines of action. At a further meeting, held on

May 3, it was agreed to convene the Conference of District
Trade Union officials for the following day. The District
Committee of the N.U.R. had also taken similar action,
and the first formal meeting of the Central London Strike
Committee was held at Headland House, Grays Inn Road,
on Tuesday, May 4. The Secretary of the London Trades
Council was appointed Secretary of the Strike Committee.
Due to the state of disorganisation, and the T.U. officials
having to attend to their own domestic problems, nothing
in the way of organisation was agreed upon. On the
instructions of the T.U.C., the Union representatives
covering the Distributive and Transport Trades were
formed into a Permits Committee, and commenced operations almost at once. Formal endorsement of the functions
of the Central London Joint Strike Committee was secured
at a meeting with the Sub-Committee of the General
Council on Friday, May 7. The General Council also
agreed to the appointment of one of their number as a
Liason Officer to keep contact between the General Council
and the Central London Strike Organisation. Up to the
last day of the strike this functionary never materialised.
This fact considerably hindered the work of the London
movement. It may also here be noted that the Secretary
of the London Labour Party at first attended the meetings,
but did not maintain contact, and he was subsequently
put in charge of the Transport Arrangements at Eccleston
Square. The following was the Constitution on which
we worked :—

1. *Name.*—Central London Joint Strike Committee.

2. *Composition.*—All District Secretaries or their representatives
of London Trades Unions affected by the Strike, in conjunction
with the E.C. of the London Trades Council.

3. *Function.*—To co-ordinate the efforts of all Local Committees
or Councils of Action in the London and Greater London Areas.

4. *Meetings.*—To meet at 3 p.m. daily at Headland House,
308 Gray's Inn Road, W.C.1.

5. *Executive Committee.*—The Chairman, Secretary, Assistant
Secretary, and two other members to act as an Emergency Committee between Council meetings.

Special points.—Due to the nearness of Eccleston
Square, the work in London was very badly handicapped.

Each Union District Committee or Council had their all-day sittings. The General Council created a separate Power Gas and Electricity Committee apart from the London Movement. The General Council then issued instructions that the only permits to be recognised were those issued from Unity House, and because of this state of affairs the Central Strike Committee largely resolved itself into an Advisory Body, issuing leads on various matters but without any power to implement their advice or instructions. The work of co-ordination largely resolved itself into convening meetings of delegates from local Councils of Action, receiving reports from Unions and Strike Committees, and issuing advice on lines of work. It can be said that the organisation was of the most unsatisfactory character, and is now being remodelled against any possible repetition of a General Strike. Strong efforts are being made to create a machine for London which will be able to overcome the difficulties experienced during the Ten Days. No effective contact was maintained either with the Local Councils of Action or Strike Committees.

Arrangements with Co-op.—On April 8, the London Trades Council adopted the following resolution :—

" To press the T.U. Congress and Co-operative Union for an immediate decision as to a joint working arrangement in the event of an industrial dispute arising out of the present mining crisis.

In the meantime we instruct the Trades Council Executive to approach the Management Committees of the principal Co-operative Societies with a view to at once instituting a joint publicity campaign and raising special local funds for this and dispute purposes.

The Publicity Campaign to be ranged around the following points :—

1. The Coming Industrial Struggle.
2. Every Trade Unionist a Co-operator.
3. Every Co-operator eligible a Trade Unionist."

But it was not possible to develop this policy before or during the strike. No contact at all was established with the Co-operative Movement in the London Area.

Preparations for the future.—In view of the weakness of the organisation during the General Strike, the London Trades Council set up a Committee to investigate and report ; the main recommendations made are given below :

We regard the problems of the situation as coming under three headings :—
    (a) Organisation.
    (b) Publicity, Propaganda and Agitation.
    (c) Finance.

We recommend that certain Committees be set up from amongst the Delegates, with a member of the E.C. as Chairman or leader of each Committee, and responsible to the Executive and Council for the right direction of his Committee.

Such Committees to consist of at least seven members.

Amongst such Committees we recommend :—

1. An *Organising Committee*, to be responsible for (a) sending deputations and speakers to affiliated and non-affiliated working-class organisations in London for the purpose of strengthening and more closely linking the organisations already affiliated, and securing the affiliation of the non-affiliated ; (b) generally superintending the work of building up and strengthening the L.T.C. ; (c) doing the requisite organisational work entailed in the holding of conferences, great mass demonstrations, etc. ; (d) assisting in the organisational work of affiliated organisations, particularly the Trades Councils, and in campaigns for 100 per cent. trade unionism, and the formation of factory committees and workshop organisation.

2. A *Publicity, Propaganda*, and *Agitational Committee*, whose functions shall be to (a) secure as much press publicity for the activities of the London Trades Council as possible ; (b) prepare and issue all public statements, leaflets, manifestoes, reports, etc., of the Council; (c) issue, when means permit, a bulletin dealing with the Council's work ; (d) prepare and issue speakers' notes and propaganda material ; (e) establish a panel of speakers of all those delegates who do public speaking, and arrange for their fixtures and generally superintend their work ; (f) have jurisdiction over, and use to the utmost advantage, such platforms, banners, etc., as may be in the possession of the Council ; (g) seek every opportunity of raising important propagandist and agitational issues, both in the Council and its affiliated organisations, and especially stimulate and centrally help

forward the propagandist and agitational efforts of local Trades Councils.

[3] A *Committee for Raising Finance*, whose functions shall be, in conjunction with the Treasurer, to seek every means of improving the finances of the Council.

4. A *Social Purposes Committee*, whose functions shall be (a) to arrange for the holding of social functions, such as Re-Unions, Concerts, Whist Drives, etc. ; (b) the organisation of sports of various kinds, etc.

5. A *Women's Committee*, whose functions shall be to (a) specially stimulate interest in the organisation of women workers in their respective unions ; (b) emphasise the special claims of women in the work of the Council ; (c) devise means of interesting working women generally in the work of the Council.

Subsequently, as the L.T.C. extends its activities, we urge that special committees be appointed to deal with the organisation of the Youth, work in connection with the Co-operative Organisations and Unemployment.

We believe that the time is rapidly approaching for the extension of the constitution of the L.T.C. so as to include all the organised forces—Co-operative and Political as well as Trade Union—of the working-class movement in London. And we do earnestly recommend that the closest immediate contacts be established with :—

(a) The London District Councils of all the Trade Unions in the Metropolis.

(b) The Metropolitan Co-operative Organisations.

(c) The Workmen's Clubs.

And, further, that a *Political Committee* be established to deal with all essentially political matters arising in the Council, our work in regard to the London Labour Party, and matters dealing with public authorities, Borough Councils, Boards of Guardians, L.C.C., Rota Committees, etc.

Lowestoft and District.

Organisation.—As Council of Action. Not being maintained, except that Trades Council will form nucleus of Strike Committee if necessary.

Arrangements with Co-op.—Co-op. willing to supply goods if arrangements were made by Trade Unions E.C.

Publicity.—Local bulletin issued—1000 copies—every day during strike and is still being issued when required by printers who have been victimised.

Position on May 12.—No sign of weakening.

Llandudno.

Organisation.—We were not called upon to act in any way. The Strike Centre was at Llandudno Junction. Railwaymen only in this district.

Arrangements with Co-op.—None necessary.

Publicity.—No local sheet issued.

Position on May 12.—One man had gone back to work (Railway Guard).

Macclesfield.

Organisation.—As Council of Action, including T.C. and Strike Committees.

Arrangements with Co-op.—Banking arrangements ; also the local Co-op. was very reasonable and helpful in regard to assistance in cases of distress.

Special Points.— (a) Two sessions per day, morning and afternoon, were held at the commencement of the strike, principally to interpret instructions received by affiliated Trade Unions from their respective head offices. Usually the T.U. concerned was prepared to give its unbiassed view and recommendation, but the general discussion proved that all concerned were really anxious to do all in their power to bring the strike to a successful issue. (b) The Building Trades responded wholeheartedly to the " call," and the only weak spots were Plumbers and Painters. (c) The A.E.U. did not respond locally until pressure was applied.

Position on May 12.—No sign of weakening.

Mansfield.

Organisation.—Trades Council Executive, with delegates from all Trade Unions affiliated and Labour Parties, etc. The special organisation is now left in abeyance.

Arrangements with Co-op.—None.

Special points.—The occasion was too big for the local machinery to cope with, and fresh duties were allotted to committees reporting to a central committee.

Publicity.—Local bulletin issued for 8 days—about two dozen daily. Not being continued.

Position on May 12.—No sign of weakening whatever.

Methil.

Organisation.—The Methil and District Trades and Labour Council formed itself on May Day into a Council of Action, organised into the following sub-committees :— Food and Transport, Information, Propaganda, and Defence Corps. To these there were later added Entertainments and Class-War Prisoners' Aid. Each sub-committee had its own convener, and there was a convener of all committees, a sort of " convener-general," who was, in effect, the chief executive officer of the Council of Action.

Food and Transport.—This committee was charged with the organisation of communal feeding (though this did not come into operation till after the general strike) and the whole system of transport permits. Permits were only issued to trade unionists, and the Council's control was very complete.

Information and Propaganda.—For its courier service the Council had three motor cars, 100 motor cycles, and as many ordinary bicycles as were necessary. These worked under the Information Committee, covering the whole of Fife, bringing in reports, taking out information, and carrying speakers who were everywhere in demand. Speakers were sent as far north as Perth ; a panel of 30 speakers was drawn up (they went in threes—a miner, a railwayman, a docker) and speakers' notes were issued by the Propaganda Committee. A daily news bulletin was duplicated. There were daily meetings and demonstrations.

Defence Corps.—At the beginning, the Workers' Defence Corps comprised 150 men, but this rose to 700 after police charges on pickets. The area was patrolled by the Corps, organised in companies under ex-N.C.O.'s, and there was no further interference by the police with pickets.

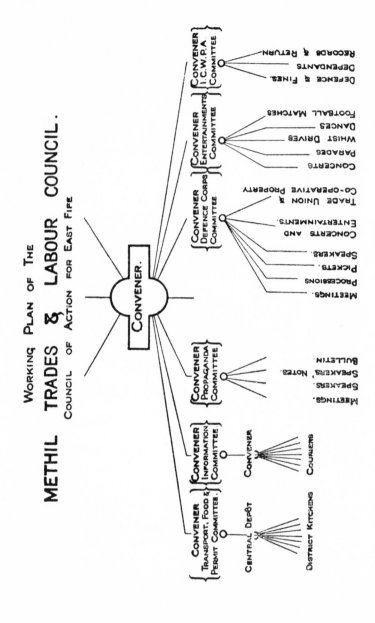

Working Plan of The

METHIL TRADES & LABOUR COUNCIL.

Council of Action for East Fife

CONVENER.

- Convener Transport, Food & Permit Committee.
  - Central Depôt
  - District Kitchens
- Convener Information Committee
  - Convener
  - Couriers
- Convener Propaganda Committee
  - Meetings.
  - Speakers Notes.
  - Speakers
  - Bulletin
- Convener Defence Corps Committee
  - Meetings.
  - Processions.
  - Pickets.
  - Speakers.
  - Concerts and Entertainments.
  - Trade Union & Co-operative Property.
- Convener Entertainments Committee
  - Concerts
  - Parades
  - Whist Drives
  - Dances
  - Football Matches
- Convener I.C.W.P.A Committee
  - Defence & Fines.
  - Dependants
  - Records & Return

Mexboro'.

Organisation.—As an Emergency Committee, working in conjunction with the T.U.C. Not being maintained.

Arrangements with Co-op.—None.

Special points.—Splendid chain of communication, but too many dispatch riders. This department needs careful study, as it is an indispensable department in times of a strike.

Publicity.—The issuing of a bulletin in Mexboro was not necessary, because our immediate neighbours at Rotherham, Doncaster, Barnsley, and Sheffield, were very active in this way of disseminating news. The bulletins became a target for the police, therefore in future every care should be exercised in their publication.

Middlesbrough.

Organisation.—Strike Committee formed, consisting of Trades Council E.C. and two members from each strike committee. No definite arrangements for continuance.

Arrangements with Co-op.—None.

Publicity.—No local bulletin issued ; we merely posted up circulars sent out by the T.U.C.

Arrests.—One member of Strike Committee, who was also Secretary of Local Communist Party, charged with issuing a circular likely to cause disaffection, and making a seditious speech—2 months' imprisonment. About half-a-dozen for doing wilful damage to property and rioting.

MIDDLESBROUGH CENTRAL STRIKE COMMITTEE.

Secretary's Report and Recommendations.

The declaration of the General Strike found Middlesbrough Trades Council unprepared and without the necessary organised machinery for directing strike activities. In response to recommendations from several bodies, a Joint Meeting of the Executives of the Trades Council and the East, West, and Borough Labour Parties was held on Tuesday, the 4th of May, and discussed the need for setting up a Publicity Committee to guard public opinion against misrepresentation of the industrial dispute by the Government and the employers' forces throughout the country.   The Joint Executives agreed to constitute themselves as the Publicity Committee and proceeded to arrange a series of outdoor meetings to be addressed on the General Strike situation by our various speakers.   At the Trades Council meeting on the 5th May, the formation of this Publicity Committee was endorsed and steps were immediately taken to set up a Central Strike Committee, to be composed of the Trades Council Executive and two representatives from each Trade Strike Committee, which had already been formed.

The first meeting of the Central Strike Committee was held at the Labour Rooms, 88 Grange Road East, on Thursday, 6th May, at 3 p.m.   The decision of the Trades Council *re* the forming of a Central Strike Committee was considered, and it soon became evident that centralised strike direction was not yet practical in Middlesbrough, owing to the fear on the part of some of the delegates that it would result in what was termed " domestic affairs of individual unions being interfered with."   The terms of the Trades Council resolution, however, were modified to meet the criticism by adding further words stating that the Central Strike Committee would not interfere with the domestic policy of any union, in any other than a constitutional way.   Having regard to the discussion which took place on this point, it became evident that the Central Strike Committee could only hope to act as a co-ordinating and not a directional body at the outset, whatever may have been possible as the strike continued.

The reports received from the various delegates showed that in Middlesbrough the workers had responded most loyally to the General Council's Strike call.   It may safely be said that we have never known a strike entered upon with such enthusiasm and determination by the workers before.   The principle of unity undoubtedly animated everybody, and the T.U.C. General Council could depend upon the loyalty of the rank and file.   Even those who had not been called out were eagerly waiting instructions from their E.C.'s to down tools in order that they could take part in the great struggle on behalf of the miners. Various difficulties in bringing members of several unions out on strike were dealt with in our endeavours to maintain the united front.

The Central Strike Committee met daily at 3 p.m. for a business meeting, whilst from 8 a.m. to 11 p.m. various delegates arranged to be at the headquarters to deal with any emergency. The attendance of the delegates was not as good as it might have been, but this was no doubt due to the fact that the delegates were also members of their Trade Strike Committees, whose meetings they also had to attend.

The work of the Secretary rapidly increased, and it became necessary to appoint a Minute Secretary. Also, another room had to be engaged for secretarial work in connection with correspondence and dispatch riders. We had the valued assistance of 7 dispatch riders with motor cycles and side-cars, through whom we were able to establish connection with York, Darlington, Stockton, Haverton Hill, Hartlepool, Newcastle, South Bank, Grangetown, Redcar, Loftus, Carlin How, Skelton, Brotton, Guisbrough, Great Ayton, Stokesley. Our headquarters were far from being suitable as an effective working centre. Little or no office equipment was available until the typewriter and duplicator, belonging to the Borough Labour Party, had been commandeered by the Secretary. Consequently, the issuing of Central Strike Committee bulletins was delayed and it was not until the strike had been called off that we were ready for issuing a regular daily Strike Bulletin. Towards the end of the strike we had the assistance of two shorthand typists from the Railway Clerks' Association. We were also assisted by the staff at the offices of the Blast Furnacemen's Union in issuing strike news and duplicating " Notes for Speakers." T.U.C. bulletins, which we received, were duplicated immediately after receipt and distributed to outlying strike committees, and also posted up on a number of display boards which we had secured at various points of the town.

The financial position of the Central Strike Committee has been materially helped by a grant which was received on the 7th May from the Darlington and District Labour College (£7), whose chief concern in making the grant was to 'help the strikers in the great struggle, believing that success would be a tremendous educational force in bringing the working-class to a consciousness of their power.   The expenses have exceeded this grant, and it has been decided to ask the Trades Council to meet the deficit.   On the whole, the discussions which took place at the Central Strike Committee meetings while the strike was on were most orderly and instructive, and the experience should prove valuable to all the delegates.

On Wednesday, 12th May, a report came that the strike had been called off by the T.U.C. as a result of conversations with Sir H. Samuel, and that instructions to return to work would be issued by the various Trade Union Executives.   This method undoubtedly caused a certain amount of confusion and disappointed many who looked for an orderly return to work.   Employers began to impose new conditions, with the result that the workers refused to start until they could be assured of pre-strike conditions.

Now that the General Strike was over, the unpreparedness of the Middlesbrough Trades Council was once again felt.   The directing influence was lacking and each trade acted on its own.   Workers were again approaching the employers in sections to secure a resumption of work on pre-strike terms.   By sending out the strike instructions through the various Trade Union Executives, the T.U.C. found it much easier to maintain a united withdrawal of labour than it was by the same method of procedure to secure a united resumption of labour.   When a General Strike has been terminated, would it not be more practical if the question of securing re-instatement at the various works were under the control of the Central Strike Committee for each area ?   The bargaining power of the united front will be difficult to maintain under the method of each union approaching the employers separately.

The total number of strikers in this area was 10,964, and there were 3250 Blast Furnacemen unemployed as a result of the strike.   The conduct of the strikers was exemplary.

The following recommendations are now to be considered by the Trades Council Executive :—

(1) In the event of a General Strike, a Central Strike Committee be formed at once in Middlesbrough, composed of the Trades Council E.C. and three delegates from each Trade Strike Committee.

(2) That a Publicity Committee be formed at once, composed of the Trades Council Executive and representatives of the Borough Labour Party.

(3) That a Centralised Picket Organisation be formed consisting of the Picket Masters from each trade, to be under the control of the Central Strike Committee, and from whose headquarters picketing shall be directed.

(4) That Sub-Committees of the Central Strike Committee be set up to deal with (a) Dispatches, (b) Strike Bulletins, (c) Entertainments.

(5) That one or two persons be appointed who will undertake to arrange the defence of any member who may be arrested for strike activity.

(6) All Trade Strike Committees be requested to send daily report to the Central Strike Committee, and also report number of their members on strike.

(7) Publicity Committee Speakers be urged to stress the need for maintaining order and discipline.

(8) The Trades Council should provide itself with a Hand-Printing Press for emergency publicity work.   During a strike it would be invaluable.

(9) The Central Strike Committee should remain in continuous session adopting a three-shift system.

(10) In order to put into practice the foregoing, it is absolutely essential that the movement locally should have headquarters of its own which ought to be faced immediately by every branch of the movement in the town.

Mountain Ash and District.

Organisation.—Council of Action, including Trades Council E.C. and Strike Committees.   It is being maintained until the end of the stoppage, when the continuance will be further considered.

Arrangements with Co-op.—None.

Special points.—A large number of motor cyclists volunteered as dispatch riders.   Entertainment Committees were set up in each place, which provided all kinds of entertainments.

Publicity.—No local bulletin issued.

Position on May 12.—No sign of weakening whatever. Everyone was disappointed that the strike ended without a miners' settlement.

Newark and District.

Organisation.—Trades Council met every night to receive T.U.C. bulletins and convey any information to workers.   No permanent arrangements made.

Arrangements with Co-op.—None.

Publicity.—N.U.R. and R.C.A. issued three bulletins and had the strike continued A.E.U. would have joined in with them.

Position on May 12.—Printers had returned to work on previous Monday.

Newhaven and District.

Organisation.—Joint Strike Committee. This committee has not been dissolved.

Arrangements with Co-op.—The use of their hall was at our disposal all through the strike.   Advanced cash pending arrival of cheques.

Special points.—Sports and Games Committee formed ; organised marches to neighbouring towns, which assisted in the keeping up of the morale of small parties.   Excellent assistance from the local police.

Publicity.—No local sheet issued.

Position on May 12.—No sign of weakening ; everyone remained solid.   There were 888 on strike out of a population of 6000, which figure includes women and children.

Newport (Mon.).

Organisation.—Council of Action, comprising E.C. of Trades Council, E.C. of Labour Party, and representatives of each Industrial Group.   This can be called together at any time.

Arrangements with Co-op.—None.

Publicity.—Local bulletin started on May 6th.   Eight issues, 800 each.   Not to be continued.

New Tredegar.

Organisation.—The Trades Council convened a joint meeting with the Local Miners' Lodges. A representative Committee was selected from a mass meeting of Trade Unionists to act as Strike Committee. The miners have now complete control of strike arrangements, about 90 per cent. of the Trade Unionists within our area being miners.

Arrangements with Co-op.—The local Co-op. Society has decided to give credit to their members to a limited amount.

Special points.—The most notable point was the remarkable feeling of sympathy by all other trade unionists with the lower-paid miners. A keen desire to see the thing through to a successful conclusion was everywhere noticeable.

Publicity.—No strike sheet or bulletin was issued, but a very efficient despatch system was adopted to keep in touch with large centres.

Newton Abbot and District.

Organisation.—Trades Council formed themselves into a Council of Action with all unaffiliated unions co-opted and acted as Advisory Committee to the various Strike Committees.

Arrangements with Co-op.—None.

Special points.—Previous to the strike being called off, we were well organised with despatch riders up and down to London and calling at the various stations on the road, and we were well linked up in the district.

North Kensington.

Organisation.—Council of Action composed of nine members, and in addition to, but subordinate to, this Council of Action, there operated a Central Strike Committee, composed of Secretaries of affiliated Trade Unions. This met every day. No permanent arrangements made.

Arrangements with Co-op.—None.

Publicity.—Local bulletin started 11th May, issued four days—approximately 600 each issue.

Position on May 12.—No sign of weakening.

Northampton.

Organisation.—Trades Council resolved into Council of Action.   Executive Committee met each evening to receive reports from committee, which consisted of a member from each of unions affected, and sat in permanent session. Trades Council E.C. decided policy.   No special arrangements for future.

Arrangements with Co-op.—None.

Special points.—Trades Council originally intended to act as Council of Action.   Too big, and so was the committee, even with Trades Council E.C. instead of full body.

Publicity.—Duplicated bulletin issued.

Northumberland and Durham General Council and Joint Strike Committee.

Organisation.—As a result of an informal meeting on Monday evening, May 3, 1926, at the offices of the National Union of Distributive and Allied Workers, Newcastle-on-Tyne, the possibility of setting up some co-ordinating Committee for the conduct of the General Strike in the Durham and Northumberland Area (the Area of the Civil Commissioner), was discussed, and it was agreed to summon a meeting of representatives of other Unions for the next day (Tuesday, May 4).   On the Tuesday afternoon a meeting of the various Trade Union representatives was held.   At this initial meeting, the following Unions were represented :—

> Northumberland Miners' Association,
> Northumberland Colliery Mechanics' Association,
> National Union of Distributive and Allied Workers,
> Transport and General Workers' Union,
> National Union of Sailors and Firemen,
> Shop Assistants' Union,
> National Union of General and Municipal Workers,
> Boilermakers' Union,
> Federation of Engineering and Shipbuilding Trades,

Railway Clerks' Association,
National Union of Railwaymen,
Builders' Federation,

together with the—

Gateshead Labour Party and Trades Council,
Newcastle Trades Council.

After a statement had been given of the position of each Union, it was agreed to form a local General Council to cover the Northumberland and Durham area, with two representatives from each Trade Union. It was agreed, in addition, to appoint a Strike Committee composed of one representative from each Trade Union, or Group of Trade Unions, on strike or locked out. Sub-Committees were suggested both for the General Council and the Joint Strike Committee as follows :—General Council Sub-Committees : Publishing, Propaganda, Demonstration and Entertainment, Ways and Means, etc., etc. Joint Strike Committee Sub-Committees : Transport Problems, Permits, Food Supplies, Picketing.

Special points.—When Trade Unionists working under permit refused to work with blackleg labour introduced at the Docks, the Government Commissioner, Sir Kingsley Wood, approached the Joint Strike Committee with a view to establishing some form of dual control. After two meetings between Wood and representatives of the Joint Strike Committee, the latter refused to make any arrangement involving work alongside blacklegs, and all permits were withdrawn. On May 8 a Conference was held in the Gateshead Town Hall of Councils of Action, Strike Committees, etc., from all parts of the counties of Northumberland and Durham, and also from other places further afield, such as Carlisle, Middlesbrough and Workington. The actions of the Joint Strike Committee were reported and approved, but it was made clear that the Strike Committee was subject to the decisions of the T.U.C. and the T.U. Executives, and not to that Conference. The main question discussed was the position of the Co-operatives.

Arrangements with Co-op.—Considerable difficulties arose over the withdrawal of all permits, as instructed by the T.U.C., which affected chiefly the Co-operative Societies.

This problem continued unsolved throughout the strike, although partial and temporary arrangements were made to get over the most urgent difficulties. No arrangements except those relating to special permits were made.

Publicity.—On Tuesday, May 4, the Joint Strike Committee decided to take over a bulletin published by the Spen and District Trades Council. The question of printing involved difficulties owing to the instructions of the Typographical Association acting on the first instructions of the T.U.C. On Friday, May 7, it was attempted to carry out the T.U.C.'s wishes for a Newcastle edition of the *British Worker*, but it was not until three days later that the necessary arrangements could be made with the Typographical Association.

Arrests.—A number of baton charges and arrests took place in the later stages of the strike, when the authorities attempted to break up the picketing arrangements.

(*Note.*—A detailed account of the Northumberland and Durham experiences is contained in the *Labour Monthly* of June, 1926).

Nottingham and District.

Report of the Joint Advisory Dispute Committee.

Organisation.—The above Committee was constituted on May 3rd, 1926, at a meeting convened by telegram, and attended by representatives of the Miners who were then locked out, and also the Transport organisations who had received instructions to strike the same evening. It was resolved that a Joint Advisory Disputes Committee be set up, composed of two representatives from each Union involved, or likely to be involved, in the dispute, together with the whole of the members of the Trades Council Executive, such body to act in an advisory capacity. Representation was also accorded to the Long Eaton and Netherfield Disputes Committees. The Committee sat daily, as did Sub-Committees that were appointed to deal with questions of Permits, Publicity, Meetings, and Outside Pickets. No explicit instructions were received from the T.U.C. General Council and, in consequence, differences of interpretation arose, especially on questions of transport.

Permits Sub-Committee.—This Committee considered and endorsed permits for the removal of foodstuffs issued by the Joint Transport Strike Committee, and were able to render assistance in making the instructions issued by the T.U.C. General Council more effective.

Publicity Sub-Committee.—The obtaining and publication of information was dealt with and, with the assistance of comrades of the I.L.P., a daily bulletin was issued, which was both helpful and informative, and was highly appreciated. Many thousands were issued, the demand greatly exceeding the supply.

Meetings Sub-Committee.—Official meetings were held every day in all parts of the city and surrounding districts, served by a rota of speakers, and were splendidly attended. They were of valuable assistance in maintaining the morale of the men.

Special points.—Deputations waited upon the Mayor, Town Clerk, Chief Constable, Food Officer, and Coal Controller, on various matters concerned with the dispute. Deputations were received from Derby, Leicester, Loughboro', Mansfield, Newark, and many other places. Dispatch-bearers were sent to London, and also received from there, as well as towns in other counties. The Labour members of the City Council worked assiduously in encouraging the strikers, and in the maintenance of public order.

Distress.—Offers of assistance were made to provide food to necessitous cases which at the time were not needed, but have since been accepted, a notable action being the sending of ten guineas by the President of the Nottingham Cinema Owners' Association. The Labour members of the Board of Guardians, by their activity, secured the fullest possible relief for those in distress.

Ormskirk.

Organisation.—As a Labour Party, and provided housing accommodation for Strike Committees of Unions concerned.

Special Points.—Only ordinary routine of a Strike Committee.

Publicity.—Utilised bulletin supplied by Liverpool.

Position on May 12.—Some weakening in Civil Engineering section of railway, purely owing to the method of calling off the strike.

Oxford.

Organisation.—The Oxford Trades and Labour Council transformed itself into a Council of Action and co-opted representatives from the Oxford City Labour Party, the Oxford Branch of the Independent Labour Party, Students and Staff of Ruskin College, and the Oxford University Labour Club.   The organisation will be maintained in existence, through the form of a Unity Committee.   The Trades Council has reverted to its pre-strike status ; but through the Unity Committee the services of co-opted members are retained.   The Strike Sub-Committees have been revised and strengthened.

Arrangements with Co-op.—Purely as bankers.   No credit arrangements were entered into.

Special Points.—It is considered that we built up a model organisation.   Our area extended to Bletchley in the North, to Goring in the South, to Faringdon in the West, and Aylesbury in the East.   It included the towns of Chipping Norton, Witney, Abingdon and Bicester.   The detailed arrangements covering transport, speakers and finance, etc., were perfected by the students and staff of Ruskin College, whose delegates reported to the Council daily.   This Special Committee operated outside Oxford. A Meetings and Entertainments Committee was also set up for Oxford city.   It raised record sums from collections and did splendid work.   Another special feature was a Research Committee whose function was to gather and collate facts on the Mining Dispute and the Strike position as it developed day by day, and supply the same to speakers. A Publicity and Editorial Committee was set up and its work was supplemented by work at Ruskin College, the University Labour Club and the Railway Unions, viz. : Ruskin College did the research work, the University

Labour Club addressed itself to university circles, the Railway Unions addressed themselves specially to their rather widespread units. The Publicity Committee mobilised typewriters and duplicators and office equipment. All the clerical work passed through this channel. Our special plant included a wireless set.

Publicity.—A local bulletin was issued on the Thursday, and continued for nine days. The average circulation was 1200 daily. (Two and three special editions). The total output was between 18,000 and 20,000 of which nearly 12,000 were sold at 1d per copy. The balance is accounted for by free distribution in small country villages. It is proposed, after the lockout, to publish in book form (from the original stencils, which we have retained) the entire work of the Council from the original whip calling the first meeting of the Council to the final instruction to the Unions. This will include our Routine Orders. This was an attempt to build up a sort of regimental H.Q. for the Unions, so that they might know exactly what was happening both at H.Q. and in the branches.

Arrests.—None.

Position on May 12.—No weakening, Increased enthusiasm and determination. Bitter disappointment at " cave in."

Paddington.

Organisation.—The Trades Council formed itself into the Paddington Central Strike Committee, and got delegates from all bodies in the borough and every branch of the T.U., whether affiliated or not. We intend to run under our present name until the Miners are back at work, when we intend to have our T.C. work independently.

Arrangements with Co-op.—For distress only. We issued tickets to cases, who received value in food from Co-op. and we paid after.

Special Points.—Lack of any kind of rules, etc., to link up with neighbouring Council for uniformity of action.

Publicity.—We only issued a leaflet to counter one issued by Local Tory Party.

Arrests.—About 80.   Arising out of this, we appeared to be the only T.C. who formed a legal sub-committee to defend non-unionists.   We engaged Counsel and defended a few cases for the moral effect, and were in fact instrumental in getting a number off or bound over.

Paisley.

Organisation.—This Council functioned as follows :—One of our delegates was appointed on each sub-committee, *i.e.*, one member to the transport section, one to the building section, and one to the engineering section, and these sub-committees formed the Central Strike Committee for this town.   We found this plan worked pretty well, because it enabled the members to be fully conversant with the affairs of the sections, and to take back accurate reports to their own particular group of strikers.   No arrangements have been made to keep the strike machinery in operation, but it is not yet disbanded.

Arrangements with Co-op.—The only arrangements with the Co-op. here were—the use of their telephone (not free) as occasion demanded, and an accommodation they gave the local branch of the N.U.R.   The local Co-op. advanced money to the N.U.R., owing to the pay-out cheque from London being delayed.   The importance of this cannot be too strongly emphasised.

Special points.—Our local arrangements were fairly good ; our chief difficulty lay in getting accurate information from Headquarters, particularly in regard to the issuing of permits.

Publicity.—A local sheet was issued ; it started on Thursday, 6th May, and the last edition was issued on the 13th, while our circulation was roughly about 2000 per day, and gaining.

Arrests.—Only one arrest was made in this district as far as we know ; one of our comrades was fined £10 for intimidation.

Panteg.

Organisation.—As a Trades Council, acting in conjunction with a Railwaymen's Joint Strike Committee.

Arrangements with Co-op.—Distress Committee formed ; all Food Vouchers made out to Co-op.

Special points.—Very smooth and efficient working among all.

Position on May 12.—No signs of weakening whatever. In fact, there was more solidarity on the last day than on the first.

Perth.

Organisation.—Strike Committee. This is being retained as an Organising Committee—one member for each Union affiliated.

Arrangements with Co-op.—Most of the Unions were accommodated by local Society for money while waiting on cheque.

Special points.—Transport workers very poorly organised.

Publicity.—Local bulletin issued.

Defence.—Only usual pickets.

Arrests.—One member of A.S.L.E. and F. fined £3.

Position on May 12.—General disappointment about the settlement.

Plymouth and District.

Organisation.—From the commencement of the general dispute this Council acted as a Central Strike Committee in the following manner :—On the evening of the first day of the strike, May 4th, a special meeting of the delegates to the Council was held, when it was decided to set up a Central Strike Committee of—

(a) A member of the Strike Committee of each Union involved in the dispute ; and

(b) Also a representative from each organisation affiliated to our Council. In addition, our Chairman and Secretary were elected to serve in similar capacities on this Central Strike Committee, which consisted of about 50.

Out of this body a Special Emergency Committee, with executive powers, was formed, composed of 20 members. In addition each of the large Unions concerned (such as the three Railway Unions, Transport and General Workers'

Union, Building Trades Group, Engineering Group, etc.) set up their own Joint Strike Committees and dealt with their own particular matters, as far as possible, reporting their decisions to the next meeting of the Central Committee. There were also Finance, Propaganda and Sports Committees. As need hardly be explained, the function of the Finance Committee was to organise collections amongst those not called out and sympathisers, so as to enable us to assist those cases in need. The Propaganda Committee became responsible for the meetings and demonstrations held under the auspices of the Central Strike Committee, providing speakers who, in their opinion, would be best able to deal with any particular phase concerning those present. The Sports Committee were highly successful in their arrangements—concerts, billiard tournaments, card parties, cycle runs into the country districts, and football matches being arranged by them (on one occasion with the local police team, whom they defeated by 2 goals to 1—this match being played at the request of our Chief Constable, whose wife kicked off). The local clergy were approached and asked to place their Sunday Schools at the disposal of the Sports Committee, which many did very readily, and in addition daily religious services were arranged and well attended. The Special Emergency Committee, referred to above, is still in existence and is already dealing with cases of victimisation, etc., which have been brought to its notice. In addition, the other sub-committees are keeping in touch with matters affecting them.

Arrangements with Co-op.—An attempt was made by us to enlist the sympathy of the local Co-operative Society, but unfortunately the only assistance they were prepared to render was what we could pay for. (At present we are not represented on their Committee of Management, but are determined to capture it at the earliest possible moment.) The Transport Group Sub-Committee assisted the Co-op. to obtain foodstuffs, etc., from warehouses at the docks, in order that there should be no shortage of supplies, and in the second week of the strike our Finance Sub-Committee arranged with the Plymouth Co-operative Society for twenty 5/- parcels to be supplied to distress cases, on the recommendation of Trade Union Branch Secretaries, and these parcels have been paid for.

Special points.—We were fortunate in being able to work together throughout the dispute without any appreciable friction, the chief difficulty experienced being in the obtaining of direct instructions from the T.U.C. General Council in respect to matters affecting general workers, building workers, etc. ; it happened on more than one occasion that the local organiser of the N.U.G. and M.W. would receive certain orders from his Head Office before the Workers' Union organiser, and we had to communicate with the General Council on the matter before being able to advise what action should be taken, resulting in a delay of at least two hours.   We consider steps should be immediately taken to ensure that, in future, all such instructions should be co-ordinated before being issued to any one particular organiser, particularly when there are other organisations catering for similar workers in the same town.   (I need hardly point out that our organisation was somewhat loose, but nevertheless we were able to render good service, especially to those organisations who have now decided to become affiliated.)

Publicity.—Our first strike sheet was issued on May 7th. We also had copies made of any important circulars, pamphlets, etc., received from the General Council, which were given every possible publicity.

Arrests.—There were six arrests during the dispute, all of them taking place on May 8th, when some of the inhabitants showed their resentment of the provocation caused by the unnecessary running of a skeleton tram service, not to mention the insulting remarks, etc., made by some of those riding on the trams.   Some of those arrested were imprisoned, and others fined, including women, all of them, unfortunately, having previous convictions.

Pontefract.

Organisation.—Labour Party E.C. dissolved and Strike Committee composed of Committees of 17 T.U. branches formed.   Arrangements are being made to maintain this.

Arrangements with Co-op.—None during General Strike ; Yorkshire Miners' Association will arrange as between Miners and Co-op.

Special points.—Wonderful cohesion of N.U.R. branches ; lack of co-ordination between branches in other trades.

Arrests.—Two Communists.   Tried and sentenced at Pontefract for seditious speeches at Castleford, 3 miles distant.

Pontypridd.

Organisation.—My Trades Council formed the basis of the organisation which functioned during the last fortnight.   Without waiting for instructions I sent out a special summons to the delegates and also to the Secretaries of all the Trade Unions in the district, whether affiliated or not to the Trades Council.   As a T.C. we discussed the whole matter and resolved to form ourselves into the Pontypridd Central Committee.   Then, avoiding delay, we straightway set up the following departments :—

> (*a*)   Intelligence and Publicity.
> (*b*)   Lines of Communications.
> (*c*)   Transport Permits.
> (*d*)   Picketing.

I may say that the experience gained by the Trades Council as such, in dealing with various problems previous to the General Strike, served us in good stead during its nine days' course.   The organisation is being maintained.   We have resolved to keep in session.

Special points.—I would just like to mention that the organisation we set up worked very smoothly.   Specialisation was our principle.   Much greater efficiency could be attained if all the telegrams were sent to me as Secretary of the Strike Committee instead of to the several Trade Union branches.

Publicity.—Bulletins were issued only to the extent of putting them up in prominent places, and sending to the surrounding Strike Committees.   Prior to the *British Worker* being delivered we issued, on one day only, 1000 copies of a cyclo-styled sheet at ½d each.

Arrests.—No arrests have taken place in Pontypridd yet. The police made a raid on my house on the 15th, on a warrant signed by the Chief Constable.

Porth.

Organisation.—The Ward Committee was reverted into an Industrial Strike Committee, composing two additional representatives of each organisation whether affiliated to the local Party or not. This committee was working under the instructions of a Central Body, comprising one member of each local Strike Committee, and other organisations; in turn they were under the General Council of the T.U.C. Each local Strike Committee is still in existence until the present crisis is over.

Arrangements with Co-op.—No arrangements of note were made with the Co-op. other than working with them during that period.

Special points.—The only point of note was the linking up of every Strike Committee, and the exchanging of news by a courier system, which was very successful.

Publicity.—The Central Strike Committee issued bulletins from the T.U.C., also the Local Committees issued several. The first day they were published was on May 5th, and they continued until the 13th.

Arrests.—Four Communists have been arrested in this locality. They were arrested on Saturday, May 15th. They were given two months, one month, and three weeks, and the youngest boy of 17 years of age was bound over for twelve months; they have made an appeal against that decision.

Prescot.

Organisation.—We formed a Central Committee under the Council, comprising all workers on strike.

Special points.—All groups were affiliated but the A.B.T.W.U., who were all out in the British Insulated Cables work.

Publicity.—Started a bulletin Monday 10th, and ran it until Friday, the 15th.

Arrests.—One member summoned on two charges. Fine, £3 and £2 ; member of the N.U.R.

Position on May 12.—No sign of weakening.   Sent telegram to T.U.C. saying we were prepared to support them until all men were reinstated.

Preston.

Organisation.—Central Strike Committee formed by resolution of the Industrial Section of Trades and Labour Council, consisting of representatives of each Joint Strike Committee in operation, viz. :   Transport, Engineering, Printing, and Building Trades, with Chairman and Secretary of Council as Chairman and Secretary of Central Strike Committee.   Not being maintained.   The Industrial Section of the Council will deal with matters outstanding.

Arrangements with Co-op.—Arrangements had been made with local Co-operative Society for an extended credit scheme to members, with approved officials of Societies as guarantors.   This scheme was not proceeded with on account of strike ending.   Also, arrangements made for distribution of coal to members of Co-op. by voluntary labour found by Transport organisation.   System of relief vouchers instituted for cases of distress, available at any branch of the Co-op.

Special points.—The need was being felt at the close of greater directional power being placed in hands of Central Strike Committee, rather than each branch having to obtain powers from its own Executive.   Organisation here very effective.

Publicity.—Small printed " Strike News " issued by Central Committee, printed by volunteer labour from Typographical Society, plant being loaned for purpose by small local firm.   It was discouraged by Publicity Dept. of T.U.C. General Council, and is not to be continued.

Arrests.—Six arrests made in the Borough, and about seven in outlying districts.   Three received one month, two 14 days, one withdrawn, and remainder fines.

Radcliffe and District.

Organisation.—We had a Council of Action and this was merged in the Strike Committee, to which was added representatives of each Society as they came out on strike. It is still in existence, but now calls itself the " Radcliffe and District Committee for the relief of Miners' Wives and Children," and has delegates from practically every Trade Union.

Arrangements with Co-op.—Our Co-op. is giving 200 loaves, and Bury Co-op. 100 loaves daily to the Relief Committee, and they are giving a gala day to miners' children.

Publicity.—No local bulletin issued, but we distributed the *British Worker* very freely—about 1500 daily.

Arrests.—None.   We had no trouble here except that one man, not a picket, was fined £4 for assault.

Position on May 12.—Some sections of transport were weak, but the Railwaymen were splendid, only one not out, out of 220, and he only went in on the 11th.

Ripley, Derbyshire.

Organisation.—At once called a meeting of all branches affiliated and unaffiliated, and formed Central Strike Committee.   A good response.

Arrangements with Co-op.—Free use of hall for public meeting.

Special points.—Building trades bad ; others good, also labourers badly organised.

Publicity.—Local bulletin issued, but only posted outside Committee Room and a few other places.

Arrests.—Four.   Two persons sent to prison for two months.   Two more successfully appealed.

Position on May 12.—No signs of weakening.   Everybody furious when settlement was known.

Rishton.

Organisation.—Trades Council became Council of Action, with Executive Committee.   Not disbanded, but working now as Relief Committee for miners' dependants.

Publicity.—Rishton is situate between Blackburn and Accrington.   We used the bulletins issued by Strike Committees of those two places.

Position on May 12.—No sign of weakening.   Population of Rishton, 8000.   Industry, chiefly cotton weaving ; one coal mine, one paper mill.   Miners and paperworkers were stopped.   On the 11th May paperworkers in general meeting met and re-affirmed, by four to one majority, decision to remain out.   Cotton workers were anxious to be called out.   After strike, amongst all workers *general disapproval* of abrupt termination.

Romford.

Organisation.—Local Unions concerned formed Joint Strike Committee.   Still in being and expect Trade and Labour Council to be formed.

Arrangements with Co-op.—Supplies for Relief Distress obtained and special discount allowed.

Publicity.—Local news-sheet issued May 5, for 7 days. About 100 copies each issue.

Position on May 12.—No sign of weakening.

Rutherglen.

Organisation.—As Trades Council, with representatives of bodies not affiliated, such as Unemployed Committees, etc., also part of Council of Action for Lanarkshire.   Council of Action still in existence.

St. Albans and District.

Organisation.—The Trades Council invited two delegates from each T.U. Branch (affiliated or not), Co-op. and Co-op. Educational Committee, Women's Guild, and Local Labour and I.L.P.   The Emergency Committee was subsequently turned into Miners' Relief Fund Committee.   Further arrangements to be made later.

Arrangements with Co-op.—The Co-op. was asked to give credit.

Special points.—The Emergency Committee did not sit at night.

Publicity.—No local bulletin.
Position on May 12.—Very slight weakening.

St. Marylebone.

Organisation.—Emergency Committee formed. Strike and Relief Committees.

Arrangements with Co-op.—Parcels value 2/- made up and distributed, paid for out of money collected by Relief Committee.

Special points.—Too many Unions catering for same class of work.

Publicity.—Local bulletin issued from May 6, for 8 days.

Position on May 12.—Some weakening, except N.U.R., E.T.U., and Enginemen's and Firemen's Union.

St. Pancras.

Organisation.—At a Special Meeting of the E.C. of the Trades Council, held on Monday evening, May 3, it was decided to invite representatives of the local Strike Committees to form, together with the E.C., the St. Pancras Council of Action. This body met daily throughout the strike, and the officers were practically in continuous session. As a result of the strike experience, the Council is developing the organisation by industrial groups, on the lines of the T.U.C. model rules.

Arrangements with Co-op.—At the request of the Trades Council, the Co-op. agreed to supply goods on credit for a canteen which was being organised by the Women's Committee, but the strike ended before any use could be made of this.

Special points.—(*a*) Concerts and dances, etc., arranged as often as possible ; (*b*) Labour Guardians in attendance to give advice in connection with relief ; (*c*) Women's Committee set up, with representatives from Women's Sections, Co-op. Guilds, etc., to organise meetings and entertainments for strikers' wives ; held very successful meetings and was organising canteen when strike ended ; the committee has been maintained to co-ordinate collections, etc., for miners, and also to develop local T.U.

organisation of women ;   (d) Relief Committee formed to raise funds for legal defence and maintenance of families of men arrested.

Propaganda.—An agreement was made with the local Labour Parties, I.L.P., and Communist Party, to run all meetings jointly under the auspices of the Trades Council. In this way almost continuous meetings were held throughout the area.

Publicity.—A Press Committee was appointed on May 3, and from Tuesday, May 4, the *St. Pancras Bulletin* appeared daily (two pages, ½d) in two editions during the first few days, each edition running to between 4000 and 5000 copies, which were readily sold at Strike Committee Rooms and in the streets.   At a meeting of the Trades Council on May 15, it was decided to continue the *Bulletin* as a weekly.

Arrests.—A large number of arrests took place in the course of police charges in the streets ;   one man arrested for having *Workers' Bulletin* ;   Secretary of Council of Action fined £10 for paragraph in *St. Pancras Bulletin.*

Defence.—Additional pickets were placed at certain depots ;   and a Vigilance Corps was set up, which, however, was not large enough for effective use.

Position on May 12.—No weakening ;   great disappointment at end of strike and method of ending it, which caused great difficulties, especially among railwaymen.

Selby.

Organisation.—Trades Council, in conjunction with Strike Committee.   Now stands adjourned.

Arrangements with Co-op.—For use of Lecture Hall *ad lib.*

Special points.—Police assistance could not be improved upon ;   our strike police and local police worked in complete harmony.

Publicity.—Local bulletin issued from second day to May 12th (12 in all).

Position on May 12.—One boy had returned, but no adult.

Sheffield.

Organisation.—Immediately the Strike decision was made and the instructions issued to the various Unions for the withdrawal of their members, the Executive Committee of the Trades Council, at its meeting on the 4th May, agreed to defer all ordinary business, except such as was of a special character, and to centre upon creating the necessary local machinery to enable them to conduct the affairs connected with the strike in the city, and to carry out the instructions which may be issued from time to time by the General Council. It was resolved to immediately transform the Industrial Section of the Executive of the Council into a Central Dispute Committee, and to issue a circular to a number of the Unions involved, inviting them to appoint two of their members to act upon the Central Committee ; how necessary this was, events rapidly proved. It soon became apparent, that it would be necessary for the Central Committee to remain in constant session, and to enable this to operate, a series of rotas were formed, thus enabling a section to be on duty at all times, whilst not keeping any one member longer than three hours, with the exception of the chief officers, who were in the nature of things required to be present right through the day. One of the first matters to be dealt with was the position of the Railway Unions; for the first time in its history the Railway Clerks' Association was engaged in a large strike, and manfully did their members respond to the call. It was felt that with the lack of experience in strike matters, their position would be weak unless they were in close co-operation with the other Railway Unions, and even though this did not operate, it was felt that it would be a tragedy if three Railway Unions were to each have their separate Strike Committees, and be working independently of each other, and in order to prevent this, and to consolidate the movement, efforts were at once made to create a combined Railway Strike Committee, the three Unions being approached for this purpose with some success.

Issue of Permits.—On the second day of its activity,

the Central Committee found that it would be necessary to control the issue of permits to move certain goods ; it must be borne in mind that it was the expressed desire of the General Council that all essential public services must be maintained with the exception of the running of the Car Service, and the Committee undertook this duty. Permits were issued to the Co-operative Societies in the city to remove their stocks of coal.   It was found that the only large body affected in the city were the Co-operative Societies, whose employees were organised practically 100 per cent. ; the other large employers were in a happier position, as judged from their viewpoint, their men remaining unorganised, and thus the Co-operative Societies were placed at a grave disadvantage ;   this, it was felt, was not the intention of the General Council, and. the Committee did not hesitate to come to their assistance. Permits were also issued in other directions for the removal of foodstuffs, and generally these were used with discretion. It was discovered, however, in the case of one warehouse, that permits were being abused ;   where they had permits to move foodstuffs, bags of cement were being included with bags of flour, and immediately this was detected the permits were finally cancelled.   Permits were issued to small dealers for the removal of wood blocks ;   in these cases those to whom the permits were issued were men who purchased the blocks for sale as firewood, and in these cases it was laid down as a condition under which the permits were issued, that the persons concerned should not increase the price of such firewood, unless the price had been increased to them beforehand ;   and further, that they should continue to retail them as before, and not to sell in bulk.   Permits were refused for the removal of building materials, unless such material was required for the use of the Corporation upon their own Housing Schemes.

Special points.—In view of the magnitude of the work involved, it was felt to be essential that we should secure additional accommodation for the Committee, and also additional secretarial help, and we are indebted to the National Union of Clerks, who placed the whole of their office accommodation at our disposal, free of cost, and to members who rendered valuable secretarial service. It will be remembered that the General Council in their circular instructed that those engaged in certain trades should be withdrawn, and that in every case, the instructions to cease work must be issued by the respective General Secretaries, the General Council laying it down quite explicitly that only those who were so instructed must cease. This instruction led to considerable confusion. Some members of local Dispute Committees were under the impression that power was vested in local Trades Councils to interpret these instructions, and where they thought wise, to call others out ; in fact there were cases where our own Committee were definitely asked to issue instructions to the members of some Unions to cease work, thus exercising a function beyond their power. This was in the main due to the fact that the instructions issued by the General Council were so vague, in so far as they did not clearly define the powers of Trades Councils, and whilst certain Unions desired that the Central Dispute Committee should exercise the powers of a local branch of the Trades Union Congress, other Unions plainly indicated that they were prepared to tell the Committee to mind their own business, and to leave the members to their respective officials. This to a certain extent militated against close co-operation, and if the strike had proceeded for long, would have had a considerably weakening effect on the general position, owing to the creation of internal jealousies. Men in some instances were instructed in error by their officials to cease work, and it was not considered expedient by the Central Committee that where such men had ceased (except in such cases as those employed upon sanitary work, etc.) that they should be instructed to return. The Committee, however, had no power to enforce this opinion and it resolved to send a special deputation to interview the General Council in London, with the express object of obtaining the permission of the General Council to keep these men out, particularly so as it was the expressed desire of the men concerned that they should be out. The deputation was also instructed to bring to the notice of the members of the General Council some of the anomalies existing in

Sheffield ; in one case, the member of one Union employed by a firm upon outside work had been instructed to cease work, whilst other members of the same Union who were employed inside had to remain at work, and to their utter disgust, were compelled to blackleg officially upon their own fellow-members. The deputation were further instructed to press upon the General Council the advisability of extending the strike by calling out other Engineering Trades, and upon arrival at London it was learned that other centres, including Coventry, had made similar representations, and that the General Council were at that time completing plans for an extension on those lines. The necessity for widening the powers entrusted to Trades Councils was also impressed upon the General Council. It would appear that the experience of the Councils in all industrial areas showed that more effective machinery would have existed if the powers of Trades Councils had been extended, and that had they been empowered to interpret the local position in relation to instructions issued by Headquarters, a good deal of misunderstanding and overlapping would have been obviated.   There was the case of a local firm (Sanderson's) where the officials of four Unions could not agree upon the terms of the telegram sent by our deputation after the interview with members of the General Council, the General Council having instructed that where men had been called out, they must remain out regardless of previous instructions.   The officials of one of the Unions held that the telegram could not be acted upon by their members, as they had not received a copy from their General Secretary ; the official concerned was literally correct, the definite instructions in the first place being that instructions to cease must come through their own General Secretaries, but this shows, beyond all doubt, the necessity for improving the machinery in this direction before another strike of equal magnitude is arranged.   The morale of the workmen concerned in this city was exceptional throughout the entire period, our chief difficulty here being, not to get the men out who had been instructed to cease, but to keep these at work whom the General Council desired should for the time being remain.

Couriers.—Contact was maintained throughout between the Committee, the General Council, and other centres by means of special couriers. Fortunately for the movement, a number of people possessing cars and other motor vehicles were in sympathy with our objects, and placed themselves at the disposal of the General Council. By this means information was oft-times obtained, not only from the General Council, but from other centres. A special Cycle Corps was organised in Sheffield, and with their help we were able to transmit what information came through from the large centres, to the area surrounding Sheffield. In addition to this, we were very fortunate in having cars placed at our disposal locally, and by the aid of those friends who were able to assist, we were able to transport several railwaymen and others who were stranded here to their homes; men were so transported as far as Manchester, Birmingham, York, and other places. In this connection be it noted, that it was felt that a number of the larger industrial centres should have been made the official centres of the General Council for the receipt and transmission of such information and instructions as could be obtained.

Publicity.—Sheffield was kept supplied with official information by the issue of a Strike edition of the *Sheffield Forward*; this was published in order to keep the public supplied with authentic news, and to check the journalistic errors which were so prevalent in the capitalist press, such as was published. A staff of volunteers working right through the night assisted the editor, who during the whole of the period of the dispute rarely got to his bed. Efforts were made to get a service of cars running in the city; the Tramways Committee authorised the taking of a ballot of their employees to ascertain who were in favour of resuming work. The features of this ballot were exposed in the *Sheffield Forward*, and a writ for libel was issued against the Officers of the Council in connection therewith, and although a nominal verdict was given to the plaintiff, the facts in connection with the taking of this ballot as explained by the *Forward* were confirmed in a Court of Law.

General Conclusions.—Arising from the strike, and

based upon the experience gained, the following conclusions have been arrived at by this Committee :—

(a) That more power should have been vested in the local Trades Councils.

(b) That in all cases they should have been made responsible for interpreting the instructions of the General Council, in accordance with the local positions, and to decide as between Unions in case of misunderstanding.

(c) That the original instructions issued to Trades Councils were too ambiguous in their character, and should have been more clearly defined in order that confusion should have been avoided.

(d) The instructions in connection with the calling out of men engaged in the Engineering Trades were responsible for some confusion. Officials in different districts gave varying interpretations in connection with the Order.

(e) We are of opinion that the instructions to cease work would have been more effective if those had been issued by the Central Authority in London, and that one at least of the Officials of the different Unions should have been stationed in London, and placed in direct co-operation with the General Council.

(f) That it is desirable that some arrangement shall be made between the General Council and the Co-operative Movement prior to another National Strike, and that the General Council should appoint a sub-committee to prepare detailed plans, based upon the experience gained since May, in preparation for any future strike, as we are convinced that adequate provision had not been made beforehand for the strike, and, whilst we believe that the General Council did very well during the twelve days that the strike lasted, having regard to the lack of definite preparation, we are convinced that a different issue would have been the result if plans had been carefully considered beforehand.

(g) A member of the General Council addressing the members of this Committee said that the General Council were determined to carry this through to the bitter end ;

they were aware that Eccleston Square might be raided, that the members of the General Council might be arrested, and that the end might mean utter bankruptcy so far as the finances of the movement were concerned, yet withal that the General Council felt that it would be better to fight on even if defeated—better utter defeat than surrender.   Yet the General Council failed to make provision for the reinstatement of the members of the Unions who had come out so magnificently in support, not of their own demand, but in support of one section of their class whose general standards were to be forced down in some cases to the coolie level unless the plans of the employers were thwarted, and what had been proven to be the most magnificent display of working-class solidarity in support of a principle was to a large degree marred by the eagerness with which the strike was ended, without consideration of the consequences to the miners' cause, and without adequate provision being made for all to return.

(h) We believe that the General Council were wise in suppressing the publication of the Capitalist Press, realising only too well how the press is invariably upon the side of the employers, and that they would not hesitate to distort their news to the prejudice of the workman if considered necessary, yet we are of opinion that efforts should have been made with the Printing Trades for the publication of Labour Papers in the various centres.

It is of no avail to weep over the past ; the future is before us, we shall only succeed provided that we do not emulate the ostrich and dig our heads in the sands, but assimilate the experience gained during the past few months, and build for the future upon the lessons which we have learned.

Sittingbourne.

Organisation.—Delegates from the nine T.U. Branches concerned locally, together with the Officers of the T.C. and L.P., formed the Central Strike Committee.   It is now collecting funds for Miners' wives and children.

Arrangements with Co-op.—None.

Publicity.—We issued extracts from the Official Bulletin, issued by the T.U.C. About 24 foolscap size issued daily in duplicated form.

Position on May 12.—Only signs of weakening with individuals here and there. Generally speaking, no.

Southall Norwood.

Organisation.—As Council of Action, composed of Industrial Section of Executive Committee of Trades Council, together with Secretary and Chairman of each Trade Union branch in the district. This is being maintained.

Arrangements with Co-op.—None.

Special points.—Each Union dealt with domestic business and reported to Council meeting each evening. Rota of motor cyclists set up with definite turns of duty. All dispatches sent through one centre to avoid overlapping. Social Committee and Distress Committee set up.

Position on May 12.—Decidedly no signs of weakening.

Sowerby Bridge.

Organisation.—As a Council of Action comprising Trades Council Executive Committee, three representatives from Societies in dispute, had full control in this area. Ready to function again if required.

Arrangements with Co-op.—None, but local Co-operative Society proposed to assist if required.

Special points.—A regular service of despatch riders organised and worked in conjunction with N.U.R. despatch riders. Council of Action in constant session and mass meetings in afternoon and concerts in the evening, open to the public.

Defence.—A few men appointed to assist in maintaining peace in the streets and highways—a huge success.

Arrests.—No arrest up to present, but expecting a charge of intimidation to be brought up.

Stafford.

Organisation.—As Council of Action, including T.C. and Strike Committees. This is being maintained.

Arrangements with Co-op.—None, except permits were given for transport.

Publicity.—Local bulletin issued from May 5th to end of strike.

Arrests.—Six.

Position on May 12.—No signs of weakening.

Stepney.

Organisation.—The Trades Council elected a Council of Action from amongst themselves, which was given power to co-opt suitable persons, viz., representatives of the Labour group on the Borough Council and Guardians, also of the Strike Committees.

Arrangements with Co-op.—None.

Special points.—Fortunately, we have control of the Guardians and Borough Council and all the latter's halls were placed at the disposal of the Council of Action. Meetings and concerts were arranged every night of the strike. Each member of the Stepney Borough Council was served with copy of an Order made by the Minister of Transport (on 11/5/26) to supply electrical energy to all consumers desiring same at all times of the day and night. Default of the Order renders each member of the Council liable, on conviction, to £100 fine or 6 months' imprisonment, or both. The Order was made under the Electricity Supply Acts and the E.P.A. As far as could be ascertained, Stepney was the only Borough that had no supply of Electricity during the day time.

Publicity.—Local bulletin issued on May 5th, 6th, 7th, 8th, 10th, 11th. 3000-6000 each issue.

Arrests.—One, the Secretary of London Jewish Bakers' Union, in connection with a local strike that they had on at the time. He was arrested for intimidation.

Stirling and District.

Organisation.—Scottish T.U.C. Centre as Trades Council, Strike and Transport Committees.

Arrangements with Co-op.—None.

Special points.—Co-ordination among Transport and Railway Unions good ; other Unions kept apart.   Miners active on road ; picketing in district.

Arrests. — Four railwaymen ;   numerous arrests in immediate district.

Position on May 12.—Some weakening apparent, except among railwaymen.

Stockport.

Organisation.—Set up Industrial Committee, including Transport and Engineering.   Provided Speakers' Panel ; arranged concerts, etc.   Placed organisation at disposal of Strike Committees, also material.   Staff issued bulletin, 7200.   Industrial Committee is being maintained in existence.

Arrangements with Co-op.—None.

Special points.—Supplemented and assisted Central Strike Committee without reservation.

Publicity.—Local bulletin issued.

Arrests.—Secretary, Communist Branch.   Given one month, after searching his house, not arising out of strike action.

Stockton and Thornaby.

Organisation.—As Joint Strike Committee.   The full scheme of organisation in force towards the end of the strike is given below.

Arrangements with Co-op.—None.

Special points.—On the whole our organisation worked well, considering it was the first time anything of this sort had happened.

Publicity.—Only one bulletin issued for sale.   Bulletins were posted outside our Strike headquarters several times daily.

Stockton Organisation Scheme.

In accordance with the instructions of the General Council of the T.U.C., the conduct of a strike in the Stockton and Thornaby district is in the hands of the whole of the bodies actually participating in the dispute, working in conjunction with the local Trades and Labour Council.

As a result of the experience gained, the following organisation was developed and functioned in the various details necessary ;—

(1) *General Strike Committee.*—To consist of the Trades and Labour Council Executive Committee, Labour Party Executive, Labour Members of Public Bodies, and representatives of all Unions affected in the dispute.   This Committee shall decide questions of policy in carrying out the strike and no one shall participate in its business except upon production of the authorised credential card issued to the members.   It is understood that Trade Union members may be appointed to sub-committees without necessarily being on the General Strike Committee.   The General Strike Committee will meet at 10 a.m. daily.

(2) *Executive Committee.*—This shall consist of ten members of the General Strike Committee, along with the Chairman and Secretary of the Trades and Labour Council.   The E.C. shall deal with all questions referred to them by the General Strike Committee, and with important business arising between the meetings of the latter.   The E.C. shall meet daily at 9 a.m. and 8 p.m. and other times as may be necessary.

(3) *Transport Sub-Committee.*—This Committee shall consist of members of the Transport Unions, with a representative of the E.C., and shall be responsible for ;—

    (*a*) Arranging lines of communication by road for messages, despatch riders, etc., and appointing people to undertake these duties.

    (*b*) It shall delegate definite individuals for despatch work to each Rota Committee, and endeavour to draw up a definite time-table for despatch services each day.

    (*c*) Deal with matters referred to it by the E.C. or G.S.C.

(4) *Finance Committee.*—This Committee shall consist of the Financial Secretary of the Trades and Labour Council and other three members.

(5) *Rota Committees.*—Five Rota Committees are established to deal with business which is not covered by other sub-committees, and shall be responsible for the whole of the picket arrangements. A picket roster officer shall be appointed who will be responsible for receiving the names of all Union members prepared to take picket work.   She will be in attendance in the ground floor hall between 10 a.m. and 12 noon daily, to register the names of picket workers.   She, in conjunction with the Rota Committees, will have to prepare the full roster for each day's working.   Branch Secretaries and other Union officials must keep in constant touch with the picket roster officer and the Rota Committee.   A Tramways representative will work in conjunction with the Rota Committees, one at least being in continuous attendance.   Vacancies on the various Rota Committees to be filled by the chairman finding

substitutes.　Rota Committees have power to co-opt as necessary. Each Committee shall be responsible for providing food and other essentials for despatch riders.　To ensure uniform procedure upon each committee, the chairman of each Rota shall consult from time to time as necessary in committee, along with the E.C. member delegated to the Rota Committees.

(6) *Publicity Committee.*—This Committee, consisting of four members and E.C. representative, shall issue Strike Bulletins at least once daily : deal with false or B.B.C. reports : responsible for holding public meetings, etc., and carry out any other duties delegated to them.

(7) *Social Committee.*—This Committee shall consist of four members and E.C. representative, and be responsible for providing entertainment and developing the social side of the situation.

(8) *Clerical Organisation.*—The clerical organisation shall be established to assist the Secretary and the various sub-committees. The Secretary must be kept fully posted with all work which each sub-committee is doing, and as far as possible, all minutes of meetings must be typed, and when a sub-committee is meeting, a clerk will be supplied, if possible, to record procedure.　One copy will be retained by the sub-committee, and the other for the information of the General Strike Committee.

(9) *General Instructions.*—All correspondence, reports, etc., must pass through the General Office, and matters relating to the sub-committee will be distributed from this point, which will act as a clearing house.　Sub-committees requiring a meeting should make application to the General Office for same.　The E.C. room to be allocated where possible.

(10) *Reports as to the position.*—We should be supplied from each Branch with a brief statement of the position so far as his union is concerned, and the following should be always embodied in the daily report ;—

    1. Number of men signing the books each day.
    2. Number of men not called out, but who are out of work
        owing to the strike.

Any special comments relevant to the position, which are essential to obtain a fair and concrete review of the general position daily.

Stratford-on-Avon.

Organisation.—Trades Council and Labour Party, with Strike Committee.

Arrangements with Co-op.—Only for large meetings ; not very sympathetic with Labour Party.

Special points.—Arrangements good and carried out very satisfactorily.

Position on May 12.—No signs of weakening whatever. Solid and full of spirits.

Swindon.

Organisation.—As a General Council, consisting of representatives of all Unions, with Chairman and Secretary of Trades Council. We are still in existence.

Arrangements with Co-op.—The Co-op. Society met all our demands. They kept a store of 300 gallons of petrol in hand for supply to our despatch riders. Inaugurated a scheme whereby members could have food supplies and honoured the vouchers of our Relief Committee for food. In addition they put their meeting rooms at our disposal.

Special points.—Our organisation worked so well that it is impossible to find bad points.

Publicity.—We ran a daily bulletin, from 4th May to 17th May. It was the T.U.C. Bulletin copied off, with our district news added. We supplied all Trade Union branches and all District Strike Committees with copies. We have stopped issuing now.

Arrests.—No arrests were made here ; in fact we worked so well with the police that when our autocratic Mayor sent two tramcars on the streets the police allowed our strike leaders to take charge of the situation. This was the only incident of excitement during the whole of the strike.

Tonbridge.

Organisation.—Trades Council Executive called special meeting and worked in conjunction with organisations affected by forming Central Strike Committee. This is not being specially maintained, but whole of organisations in dispute are affiliated and constantly in touch.

Arrangements with Co-op.—None. Supplies in town were plentiful.

Special points.—Entertainments, public meetings, whist drives, football and cricket matches, etc., etc., realised nearly £90, which has been utilised for relief of distress. There were ten organisations affected, representing 924 members, but actually on strike there were 1137, plus two non-affiliated organisations with membership of 8 and 7 respectively, and it is expected that at least one of these will apply for affiliation at next Trades Council meeting.

Tunbridge Wells.

Organisation.—As an Industrial Committee, with two delegates from each Trade Union involved in strike. It continues in existence as an Industrial Committee, with delegates from all Unions.

Arrangements with Co-op.—Tunbridge Wells Co-operative Society gave credit on orders for goods. All goods, however, are now paid for.

Special points.—Certain amount of confusion in Building trades, owing to exceptions made in calling out orders. N.U.R., A.S.L.E. and F., Plasterers, A.U.B.T.W., N.B.L. and G.W., Typists, all out 100 per cent. N.U.G. and M.W., Transport and G.W., C. and S.W. partly out. Plumbers (Sanitary workers) and House Painters and Decorators not called out.

Publicity.—Duplicated leaflets with propaganda issued most days.

Defence and Arrests.—No necessity for defence organisation here. No arrests.

Position on May 12.—No sign of weakening.

Ulverston.

Organisation.—Formed Joint Strike Committee. Worked in conjunction with Barrow-in-Furness Committee. Business pertaining to strike undertaken and couriers established. Strike events and general news supplied to us by Barrow Committee. Joint Strike Committee was maintained until May 25th, 1926.

Arrangements with Co-op.—Yes, mainly in connection with allocation of coal supplies.

Special points.—A general lack of understanding and fear of consequences particularly noticeable.

Publicity.—A bulletin was issued from Barrow from May 6th for about 7 days. Most we could obtain was 100 copies. Sold here in ten minutes.

Arrests.—None. Railwaymen ran " Band " for a few days, playing up to work Goods Agent and Traffic Inspector. Police escorted these men and finally stopped " Band." Instruments obtained from Town's rubbish tip.

Ulverston.—Special Note from Secretary.

In addition to the completed form, I feel compelled to give you a more detailed account of the happenings during the huge upheaval of recent date.   Ulverston is an old market town, its Charter dates back to 1280, and is a tory stricken place from one end to the other. We (the Trades Council) formed a " Joint Central Strike Committee," composed of all those who were implicated in stoppage, or to be more accurate, representatives of such—4 delegates from Trades Council, 2 each from Railwaymen and Transport Workers' Union, and 1 each from other bodies.   Difficulties immediately rose in regard to Blast-furnacemen, about 370 in number, as to whether they were " on strike " or " locked out."   I informed them that they would be declared " on strike," which proved correct.   This body hesitated about being associated with the Strike Committee for some time.   On receipt of the verdict from the Labour Exchange, they became openly associated with the Joint Strike Committee.   We then experienced difficulty with owners of our headquarters, the Catholic Club, regarding a bulletin board ; finally they decided not to allow us to place a board on flags in front of premises, and another 24 hours were lost in obtaining the Temperance Hall, where every facility was found.   This hall is situated right in the street where all the " dope " was disseminated from, but the end was too near at hand by this time to be of any great use to us.   Having representatives of the Printing trades on the committee, I naturally thought these men would be a source of assistance in issuing bulletins of various descriptions ; they were either afraid or incompetent, and proved useless for this purpose.   From the very beginning I could clearly see the impotency of our committee as a corporate body to hold its end up on its own.   I therefore got in touch, almost at the commencement, with the Barrow-in-Furness Strike Committee, and subsequently placed the Ulverston Committee in their hands.   Until the end we worked with them in a cordial manner.   Two days before the end we found no less than three men to act as couriers, each having a motor cycle.   I am satisfied that if the strike had lasted three months longer Ulverston would have been in working order. The men obeyed the call manfully, all industries, with one small exception, being stopped. The end of the strike is a puzzle to all here, and was called off without giving any apparent reason. Yesterday's issue of the *Herald* is a keen disappointment to all here, no mention beyond Mr. Bowerman's contribution being published. I am quite satisfied that the political weapon will receive an impetus through this great debacle.

Wakefield.

Organisation.—A General Strike Committee was set up consisting of the delegates of the Trades Council and the whole of the Trade Union Branch Committees affected by the strike. From this body a Central Strike Executive was set up consisting of the Chairman and Secretary of the Trades Council, and seven other members elected from the General Strike Committee. Group committees were also set up to cover the industries affected, viz. : Transport Group, which included all members of the Transport Unions ; Building Trades Group ; Iron and Steel Group. These Groups had matters affecting them to consider and recommend action to the Central Executive. A Picket Committee was also set up, charged with the organisation of picketing. All the activities of these different Committees were co-ordinated by the Central Executive, which was responsible for the final decisions. The General Strike Committee was called together every other day and interest was maintained throughout the whole of the period. The Central Strike Executive is still in being.

Arrangements with Co-op.—The only arrangements made with the Co-op. were for the provision of meals for our despatch riders.

Publicity.—No local bulletin issued. We were charged by the T.U.C. to publish their bulletins and speakers' notes, and distribute them over the area covered by Dewsbury, Normanton, Castleford, Pontefract, and Knottingley. This taxed our duplicating resources to the utmost.

Arrests.—None.

Position on May 12.—No sign of weakening. On the contrary, the spirit was magnificent, and consternation and dismay prevailed when the news that the strike was called off had been confirmed.

Watford.

Organisation.—As Central Strike Committee, with representatives from Trades Council and each Union affected. President and Secretary of T.C. acting in similar capacity to Central Strike Committee. As outcome of experience, T.C. is forming Industrial Committee.

Arrangements with Co-op.—Credit given by Co-op. to members equivalent to their usual weekly purchases.

Special points.—Local T.U. and Labour Club placed Club and Hall at disposal of Committee—no charge made. Refreshment Buffet organised. O.C. Lines of Communication set up in sole charge of despatch riders.

Publicity.—Local bulletin issued for four days, from May 10, and final issue May 21.

Arrests.—Two busmen for interfering with " volunteer buses."

Position on May 12.—No weakening.

Wednesbury.

Organisation.—Trades Council acting with affiliated Trade Union branches.

Special points.—The Council is now looked upon as a greater factor, particularly by political parties.

Publicity.—Bulletin issued each Sunday ; copies sold, 750 first Sunday ; 1000 second Sunday.

Position on May 12.—No weakening. The position was magnificent. The trouble has been since the termination.

West Ham.

Organisation.—A meeting was called from 110 branches of Trade Unions in West Ham, from which a Committee of 20 was appointed to serve with the E.C. of the above Council, as Central Strike Committee for West Ham, having daily contact with every Strike Committee in the area. Arrangements are being made to keep a part of this organisation in existence.

Arrangements with Co-op.—None.

Special points.—Considerable difficulty was experienced by the committee in sifting items of information in their order of truth and importance ; there was a tendency to collect all items of news, and in the absence of a supply of authentic news from the centre, this news so collected assumèd undue importance. The question of permits became complicated locally, as ' a result of the central breakdown in that department. The general question of lines of communication only began to be settled satisfactorily towards the close of the strike, and this matter will continue to have more serious attention.

Publicity.—A Strike Bulletin was issued every day, and had a circulation of 150 copies to Branches and Strike Committees.

Arrests.—So far as can be ascertained no more than six arrests were made in the area, and for minor offences only.

Willesden.

Organisation.—As a Council of Action, composed as under :—The Borough Party E.C. plus one member from each T.U. Branch (whether affiliated or not). The working Council comprised the Borough Party E.C. plus one member from each Strike Centre, a total of 24 members. The Borough Party E.C. will still act as the Council of Action and will call the larger body in any emergency.

Arrangements with Co-op.—For strike pay (banking). The relationship between the Co-op. and the T.U. movement needs drastic attention.

Publicity.—Local bulletin issued 8 days. A duplicated typed sheet, 500 each issue. We are endeavouring to issue a monthly sheet.

Defence and Arrests.—A " Maintenance of Order Corps " was formed, about 200 strong. Their assistance was recognised by the local police. Not one arrest was made in Willesden.

Position on May 12.—No weakening. There were, however, several serious questions arising which may have speedily altered the position.

Wolverhampton.

Organisation.—As Emergency Committee ; see detailed report below.

Arrangements with Co-op.—Holding meeting in Co-op. Hall.

Publicity.—Local bulletin issued from Wednesday, May 5th, for 6 days. 500 each issue.

Position on May 12.—No weakening whatever.

Report of Wolverhampton Emergency Committee.

On Monday, May 3rd, a Special Executive Committee of the Trades and Labour Council was held to consider the Coal Crisis, and an Emergency Committee of three was appointed, with full powers to co-ordinate the activities of the Unions involved, and such Committee to sit continually during the day.

The first call was made to the Transport men numbering about 3500, the Typographical Association, N.A.T.S.O.P.A., E.T.U., and some members of the A.E.U. and Allied Trades and Building Trade Workers.

An Emergency Committee was set up immediately consisting of a representative from each of the Unions so affected. The first meeting was held on Tuesday, May 4th, at 2.30, and the first problem the Committee had to face was interpreting the general circular sent down by the Trades Union Congress, together with the waiting of instructions from Unions to cease work.

An impression existed among some members of the Emergency Committee that they, the Emergency Committee, had full power to call out all workers, irrespective of official instructions, but we think the Sub-Emergency Committee was quite right in taking the point of view that their duty was not to give instructions to cease work, but that they should only carry out the wishes of the General Council, and endeavour to obtain concerted action in the bringing out of men, but even this was very difficult owing to each Union sending down different circular letters to their branches, this being most evident in the Building trades.

The Central Emergency Committee met every afternoon at the Labour Rooms, and a Strike Committee was formed of the railway groups, which met at North Road Club daily with a Sub-Emergency Committee meeting in the Labour Rooms each morning at 11 o'clock, consisting of the four appointed by the Trades Council, with a representative each of the Building Trades and of the North Road Joint Committee.

The next problem was that of communication, and the lack of reliable information, and we fixed up a communicating line between Wolverhampton and Birmingham to Stafford, Stone, and Manchester to the North, and Wellington and Shrewsbury for Chester and North Wales.   Despatch riders were fixed up with willing volunteers, and one member was appointed by the Sub-Emergency Committee to act on behalf of the T.U.C. for all the towns between Dudley and Oswestry, receiving a report each day from each Strike Committee, sending out official information from the T.U.C., supplying them with speakers where necessary, and forwarding information to London to the General Council.

As there were no newspapers, your Committee decided to issue their own Strike Bulletin, which was commenced on Wednesday, May 5th, and published every day until the General Strike was called off, and, judging by the great demand made for the copies, the publication must have served a very useful purpose.

Open-Air Meetings were arranged every day at the Market Place with a good supply of local speakers, assisted by the Miners' representatives from Cannock, and during the week-end we were favoured by the visit of several national speakers.   Sunday evening over 2500 people attended the Theatre Royal.   An overflow meeting was held at the Co-operative Hall, with 1100 people in attendance, but even with those two halls packed, thousands were unable to obtain admission.

Engineers.—The first instructions sent down to your Committee *re* Engineers were very vague, and there existed much difference of opinion between the members of your Committee as to whether they applied to the Motor industry, but eventually the Vehicle Builders received definite instructions for the withdrawal of their men.   Other Unions involved then acted in accordance with the principle which had been laid down by the General Council that if any Executive Committee of any Union had given instructions to withdraw any men in any particular factory, all other Unions were to come out as well, so your Committee very quickly succeeded in arriving at a policy which caused a complete stoppage of the Motor industry in this town.

The Building Trade had many complications.   Instructions were received by some of the Unions that all Building Trade workers should cease unless engaged upon Housing, Hospital, and Sanitation. This caused a great deal of dissatisfaction in the Building trade. The whole of the workers were determined to stand by the miners, and it was with the utmost difficulty that your Committee was able to keep within instructions laid down by the T.U.C.   A meeting of the Building Trade workers, held on Saturday, May 8th, instructed local officials to send a telegram asking for withdrawal of all men in the Building industry.

Your Committee also sent a deputation to the Mayor and the Town Clerk on the attitude of the mounted police, led by the Chief Constable, in their endeavour to protect a private charabanc plying for hire over the routes of the Transport Committee. Your deputation pointed out that it was illegal, and succeeded in obtaining the withdrawal of the private charabanc. They also dealt with many other serious complaints, but got very little satisfaction from the Mayor.

The question of the Power Station at Commercial Road also received a great deal of attention. The T.U.C. had wired asking your Strike Committee to try and come to some arrangements with the Electrical Engineer only to supply such services as house, street, and shop lighting, social services, etc., power for the production of food, bakeries, domestic purposes, and laundries, but the management refused to agree to the request of the deputation, and later, instructions were received from the T.U.C. to withdraw all men from the Power Stations.

On Monday, May 10th, it was estimated by the Manager of the local Labour Exchange that 35,000 workers had ceased work in Wolverhampton, and the Trades Union movement are indeed to be congratulated upon the splendid stand made on behalf of their more unfortunate brethren, the miners, and with very little exception, the whole of the workers stood solid and were prepared to fight to the bitter end, so that when the news came through on Wednesday, May 12th, that the Strike was over, it came as a shock, as the situation then looked as though it would last indefinitely.

Your Emergency Committee met the same afternoon and had posters displayed in front of the Labour Rooms advising the men not to return to work until instructions to that effect came from their Branch officials. It is just as well we took this precaution, because we found that in the Railway Department, Guy Motor Works, the E.C.C., and the Red Bus Section of the Transport Workers, these men were required to sign documents which would take away the whole of the rights which their fathers and forefathers had fought so dearly for, and it is quite evident that the employers of this country were prepared to use this crisis as a method of breaking down Trade Union bargaining. Your Emergency Committee think that the time is opportune for a strong campaign to be put forward with a view to strengthening Trade Unionism. They have found in this struggle, as in previous struggles, that the " nonner " as well as the Union man, answers the call made to him, and we think that every effort should be made at once to get all back into the Unions.

Wolverton and District.

Organisation.—Trades Council set up a Dispute Committee consisting of two from each Trade Union which worked in conjunction with full Trades Council.

Arrangements with Co-op.—None.

Special points.—Organisation was fairly good; we had local despatch riders. Local Music Hall lent to Committee free of all charge.

Arrests.—Twenty-four. Not one of these can be construed into a serious offence, yet fines were inflicted amounting to £103; this, with Counsel, has cost us nearly £200. We are, therefore, in financial difficulties; efforts are being made to pay this without defendants having to find money, as they have all been discharged from their employment—two of them over 60 years of age.

Woodford.

Organisation.—Council of Action.

Arrangements with Co-op.—Credit to extent of £20 food vouchers (five weeks).

Wood Green and Southgate.

Organisation.—As Joint Strike Committee, under the auspices of the Trades Council. All the powers of the J.S.C. have been given in full to the Trades Council to act as they deem necessary.

Arrangements with Co-op.—None were made.

Special points.—No special feature; all were working to their full capacity.

Publicity.—Issued bulletins twice daily; are taking steps to continue. Commenced issue the second day. A few copies enclosed.

Arrests.—No arrests, no trouble of a serious nature.

Position on May 12.—As most are Transport workers—rail and road in this area—there was a unanimous decision not to start on the Thursday, because of the attitude of the employers.

Yeovil.

Organisation.—In an advisory capacity set up Distress Committee to collect and relieve distress; still operating on behalf of miners. Council of Action was set up by Strike Committee. Strike Committee still in existence.

Arrangements with Co-op.—To render assistance to the Strike Committee as considered necessary.

Special Points.—The complete line of communication maintained to headquarters.

Publicity.—A Strike Bulletin was posted daily, May 6th to 12th, at headquarters of Strike Committee.

Arrests.—No arrests are known.   There was a good feeling exhibited by the town police throughout.

Position on May 12.—The position remained the same throughout, namely, 98 per cent. Railwaymen on strike ; some Printers ;   all A.E.U. members ;   Stone Masons 100 per cent.